CAN WE TALK?

soul-stirring

conversations

with God

PRISCILLA SHIRER

LifeWay Press®
Nashville, Tennessee

Published by LifeWay Press®
© 2008 Priscilla Shirer
Third printing September 2010

ISBN 978-1-4158-6542-2
Item 005146922

Dewey Decimal Classification: 248.843
Subject heading: WOMEN \ SPIRITUAL LIFE \ CHRISTIAN LIFE

Unless otherwise noted, Scripture quotations are from the New American Standard Bible®,
    Copyright © 1960, 1962, 1963, 1968, 1971, 1972, 1973, 1975, 1977, 1995 by The Lockman Foundation.
    Used by permission. *(www.lockman.org)*
Scripture quotations identified ESV are from The Holy Bible, English Standard Version®,
    copyright © 2001 by Crossway Bibles, a publishing ministry of Good News Publishers.
    Used by permission. All rights reserved.
Scripture quotations identified NLT are from the Holy Bible, New Living Translation,
    copyright © 1996, 2004. Used by permission of Tyndale House Publishers, Inc.,
    Wheaton, IL 60189 USA. All rights reserved.
Scripture quotations identified KJV are from the King James Version of the Bible.
Scripture quotations identified MSG are from The Message by Eugene Peterson.
    Copyright © 1993, 1994, 1995, 2000, 2001, 2002. Used by permission of NavPress Publishing Group.
Scripture quotations identified HCSB® are taken from the Holman Christian Standard Bible®,
    copyright © 1999, 2000, 2002, 2003 by Holman Bible Publishers. Used by permission.
Scripture quotations identified NIV are from the Holy Bible, New International Version,
    copyright © 1973, 1978, 1984 by International Bible Society.
Scripture quotations identified AMP are from The Amplified New Testament
    © The Lockman Foundation 1954, 1958, 1987. Used by permission.

To order additional copies of this resource, write to LifeWay Church Resources Customer Service;
One LifeWay Plaza; Nashville, TN 37234-0013; fax (615) 251-5933; call toll free (800) 458-2772; e-mail
orderentry@lifeway.com; order online at *www.lifeway.com;* or visit the LifeWay Christian Store serving you.

Printed in the United States of America

Leadership and Adult Publishing
LifeWay Church Resources
One LifeWay Plaza
Nashville, TN 37234-0175

CONTENTS

30 days

A NOTE FROM PRISCILLA

 **Conversations with God** was on the *New York Times* best-seller list for 139 weeks. I wanted to enhance my conversations with God, so I picked up a copy for myself. I just knew the author had recorded rich conversations with God; I was ready to be a fly on the wall of that dialogue. I was intrigued and challenged, but became unsettled as the book revealed a tolerant deity of blurred boundaries who was committed to no clear Scriptural margins. The more I read, the more stunned and disappointed I became. Not because the book wasn't interesting, but because it couldn't possibly be a real conversation with the one true God—the God of Abraham, Isaac, and Jacob.

The author was correct that God desires communion with us. In fact, this very principle separates our faith from every other "so-called" faith on the earth. We have a holy Father who desires to interact with the "un-holy." So much so that in the ultimate act of love, God allowed Himself to be crucified as payment for our sins. Through this means and no other, He saves us from eternal separation from God. Through Jesus alone we have a conversational relationship with the one true God. "Many ways" to have conversations with God don't exist. There's only One and Jesus is it!

Before Jesus became flesh, God could not have intimate fellowship with us because of our sin. When Jesus paid for our sin, He stripped away that barrier. Suddenly the Holy Spirit could actually occupy a human spirit because the holiness of God had wiped away the sin of His child. Now He offers us something even better than the physical presence of Jesus. God can now fellowship with each believer intimately and immediately wherever that believer might be. This intimacy is the deepest friendship and relationship possible, and the Spirit speaks primarily through the written Word—living, active, and personalized.

I celebrate that God has given us godly teachers. Let us not forget, however, that the same Spirit who lives in them lives in each of us. We must never become *dependent* on human teachers to fulfill the role of the Holy Spirit.

This little book is a catalyst to assist you in retraining yourself to rely on the Spirit. My prayer is that this will help equip you to look into the pages of the Scripture and hear what the Spirit is teaching as you fellowship intimately with your master.

The Bible not only establishes the boundaries into which every personal word God gives us will fall; it is the chief means of communication we have with God. Scripture is alive! As we read it, the warmth of God's breath brushes across our cheeks.

This is not your typical Bible study. In these pages, you will not find exegetical analysis of Scripture. You will find daily encouragement to dive in and swim in the rich living waters of the Word ... alone. The refreshment you find will change your life forever.

Each week will begin with a short article introducing the theme. It may challenge you or focus on a characteristic of God. That day you'll apply the article through one passage of Scripture. In the four daily lessons that follow, you will find several Scriptures related to the theme. I have given you many passages to ignite your divine dialogue. If time doesn't permit you to fully engage in each one every day, and it probably won't, don't feel guilty about just meandering in the one passage that grabs your attention. Remember, your goal is not to finish homework. It is to have a meaningful conversation with God.

At the end of each day's lesson, you will find a section called "More Conversation Starters." Also, you may notice one or two verses showing up several times. I want to allow those verses to become inscribed on your heart. I've also included group questions—topics to discuss in a small group—and at the end of each week optional extra questions you can answer in a separate journal or notebook if you desire. There are some leader notes on DVD 1 for those of you meeting in groups.

Each day, use "The Five Ps of Hearing God through Scripture." The first you should implement at the beginning of each day's study. You should apply the remaining four "Ps" to each passage during that day's devotional.

AS YOU BEGIN EACH DAY:

1. Position yourself to hear from God.

Habakkuk 2:1—Engage in solitude and silence.

Though can God speak to us anywhere and anytime, we find hearing easier when the distractions are limited. Find a spot where you can be alone, even if just for a few moments, so that you can more easily have an awareness of God's presence and an ability to hear His voice whispering to you. Don't be afraid of the silence. It is in the stillness that we get to know God best (Ps. 46:10).

Psalm 27:14—Expect God to speak.

Even if you have never heard the voice of God before, if you are a believer, you can now! Having intimate, conversational relationship with Him is a privilege that comes with being His child. Go into your time of Bible reading with an expectation that you will get something out of it. Don't limit God by your past experiences.

AS YOU LOOK AT EACH VERSE:

2. Pore over the passage and Paraphrase the major points.

James 1:25—Look deliberately and intentionally into the Scriptures.

When you read the Bible expecting God to speak, you cannot just skim the passage. You are not in a race to finish your lesson. Meander in each verse. If the passage allows, put yourself in the Scripture and see yourself in the story. If one verse seems to resonate with you, don't worry about finishing the rest, just stay in the passage and let the Spirit speak to you.

Joshua 1:8—Read slowly and meditatively.

Read the passage a few times, emphasizing different words each time. If a certain word or phrase pops out at you, don't ignore it. Stop and consider why. This is how the Spirit speaks; He causes Scripture to connect with the details of our lives.

• Consider the contexts as you pore over the passage:

Who are the major participants?

What are they doing? saying?

Where are they going?

Why is this happening?

How is this occurring?

3. Pull out the spiritual principles.

Spiritualize the major points of the verse.

What is God teaching? What is He revealing about Himself?

4. Pose the question.

Form a personally directed question from each of the spiritual principles you listed in the step above. Ask yourself, "Does my life coincide with the message of this verse? Is anything in my life contradicting this passage? What do I need to do to bring my life in line? How does this apply to my life right now?" As you ask yourself questions along these lines, permit the Holy Spirit to speak to you. Take time to listen (Eccl. 5:1-2) for His voice as you quietly consider the answers to these questions. As you sit still in God's presence, you will to hear the Spirit whispering to you: encouraging you, convicting you, challenging you, and inspiring you. Record what the Spirit is asking you to do.

5. Plan obedience and Pin down a date.

James 1:22—Plan to obey

Don't be one who hears and then does nothing with what she has heard. Record the steps that you can take immediately to begin responding to what God has said to you in the verses you looked at that day. Recall these steps throughout your day and put them into practice immediately. If obedience requires you to do something specific such as apologize to someone, record a date and time you will follow through. Let someone else know about your plan so you can be held accountable.

Here's an illustration from my "journal of conversations." I was studying John 1:36-37.

^{36}[John the Baptist] looked at Jesus as He walked and said, "Behold, the Lamb of God!" ^{37}The two disciples heard him speak, and they followed Jesus.

PORE AND PARAPHRASE

(36) John's eyes were on Jesus. John's ministry was focused on pointing out the Lamb of God.

(37) John's message resulted in an increased desire in the listeners to follow hard after Jesus

PULL OUT

(36) True ministry is one in which the minister's eyes are focused on Jesus. True ministry should be focused on calling all attention only to the Lamb of God.

(37) True ministry should encourage those who hear to desire an intimate personal experience with Jesus more than a relationship with the minister.

POSE

(36) Are my eyes focused on Jesus or someone/something else? If so, what? Do I seek to call attention only to the Lamb of God, or do I seek any for myself?

(37) When people hear my message do they want more of me, or are they encouraged to seek hard after Him?

PLAN AND PIN

When I teach Bible study next week (1/6/03) and in future ministry, I must develop messages that focus the listener only on seeing Jesus. My intention must not be to call attention to myself in any way. I want to begin to see people's interest stirred to experience more of God and less of me after hearing me speak.

The "Ps of Hearing God" helped me have a conversation with God that challenged my entire ministry. It took me two years to complete the Book of John as I carefully looked into one or two verses each day. Using these principles, my once drab quiet time and prayer life has grown into an explosion of fellowship and conversation with the Lord. These were once steps to follow, but now they are an automatic way for me to approach the Scriptures. I'm amazed how the Spirit speaks as He applies scriptural passages to the regular stuff of my daily existence. I hope you are ready to have real conversations with God as you look into the Word. You will never again be the same!

Blessings,

Priscilla Shirer

WEEK ONE
FIRE STARTER

LORD, I pray that this week my conversation about my tongue will mark my life forever. Grant me a spirit of deep revelation to see myself as clearly as Isaiah saw himself when he beheld Your holiness. Let Your Presence fall so heavily that I will behold my true self and desire restoration. And then Lord, come. Touch me with the fire of Your holiness and the soothing tenderness of Your forgiveness as I repent and yield this mouth to You. I want it to be a resting ground for Your praises. I don't want to allow complaints and criticisms to take up space that should be occupied with You. Starting today, lead me on the path to holiness.

Speak Lord, I'm listening.

In Jesus' name, **AMEN.**

"Woe is me, for I am ruined! Because I am a man of unclean lips, and I live among a people of unclean lips; For my eyes have seen the King, the LORD of hosts." Then one of the seraphim flew to me with a burning coal in his hand, which he had taken from the altar with tongs. He touched my mouth with it and said, "Behold this has touched your lips; and your iniquity is taken away and your sin is forgiven." **Isaiah 6:5-7**

DAY ONE
FIRE STARTER

No one can tame the tongue ... With it we bless our Lord and Father, and with it we curse men, who have been made in the likeness of God; from the same mouth come both blessing and cursing. My brethren, these things ought not be this way. Does a fountain send out from the same opening both fresh and bitter water? James 3:8-11

Bedtime had arrived. Jackson and Jerry Jr. snuggled up to me as I held them close before laying them down for the night. I cuddled them tightly, taking in the sweet, intoxicating aroma that all mothers seem to inhale from their children. I ran my fingers over the soft skin at the nape of their necks and the bottoms of their smooth feet while watching each engaging in his individual bedtime habits. My two-year-old lifted his shirt to rub his rounded belly, and my four-year-old raised his right hand to his mouth and poked his thumb inside. Both boys nestled into my side and prepared to wind down for the night. Seizing the opportunity to pray over them, I began to speak to the Lord loudly enough for them to hear my prayers on their behalf. After praying, I quoted several Scripture verses as affirmations, claiming their promises for my sons.

"You will love the Lord your God with all your heart, mind, and strength."
"God is for you, so who can be against you?"
"I know that God is causing all things to work together for your good."
"You are blessed when you go in and come out; when you are in the city and in the country."
"The joy of the Lord will always be your strength."
"The Lord has a plan for you that includes a hope and a bright future."
And finally ...
"You will bless the Lord at all times, and His praise shall continually be in your mouth."

My boys had heard these verses before (I'm serious about speaking Scripture over them as much as I possibly can), but today the message of that last one seemed to seep deeply into my four-year-old's soul. I heard the steady thumb-sucking sound halt abruptly as he lifted his head off of my chest and looked at me quizzically. "Mom," he said, "His praises can't fit in my mouth. My thumb is in there right now!" I laughed but then grew quiet as the significance of this young one's statement stung me deep within.

The praises of God cannot fit in a mouth that is already filled with other things.

I'm a complainer. I was born one, or maybe having struggled with it for so long, I just thought I came from the womb that way. The flame of my critical nature was furiously fanned until it burned uncontrollably and began to leave a smoky path of destruction everywhere I went and with every person I met.

Like others with the same problem, I lived in denial, unaware of this personality trait until a loved one, clothes still scorched by the heat of my mouth, sat me down and told me the truth. Proof of my misguided comments remained. The smell of fresh smoke lingered in the air and I could see the burn marks my heated comments had left behind on her tender heart. My loved one was kind yet honest. The conversation left me stunned—shocked by the self-revelation to which I had been so blinded but better after being made aware of it.

The Holy Spirit came with His strong conviction, uncovering this fleshly part of me yet sending soothing grace to cool the embers of my critical nature. "The tongue is a small member, yet it boasts of great things. How great a forest is set ablaze by such a small fire! And the tongue is a fire, a world of unrighteousness. The tongue is set among our members, staining the whole body, setting on fire the very course of life" (Jas. 3:5-6, ESV). I looked around at the life I had and saw small fires raging all around me. In most cases, I knew I'd started them.

In the days and weeks that followed, I began to feel a twinge of conviction every time a complaint or unnecessarily offered critical comment escaped my lips. Soon, I'd feel the conviction *before* I spoke the comment. The smoldering coals of criticism would sit on the tip of my tongue longing to make their escape. Then I had to decide whether to light the match and let the fire burn or submit to the soothing, cool living water of God's grace to me as I extended it to someone else. In those moments, what I knew for sure was that both things couldn't be accomplished at the same time. I had to choose to indulge one option or the other: to submit to the fleshly complaints of my tongue or to allow my mouth to be a resting ground for the praises of God. It had to be one or the other, and I was the one who had to make the choice.

"Does a spring of water bubble out with both fresh water and bitter water?" James asks (3:11, NLT). The answer is a resounding "No!" Both cannot come out of the same spigot. If we want our homes, workplaces, and friendships to be filled with the sound of God's praises coming from our mouths, then we must cleanse our palates of anything that would squeeze out its position of prominence. We must decide to guide our tongues, submitted to the Holy Spirit, as instruments to be used by God for His purposes, today and every day.

THIS WEEK, HAVE A CONVERSATION WITH GOD.

What does my mouth contain most frequently: God's praises or judgment and criticism? Is He pleased with what He hears me say to others? to myself? What "fires" has my mouth made that I need to go back and put out?

JAMES 3:8-11

8No one can tame the tongue; it is a restless evil and full of deadly poison. 9With it we bless our Lord and Father, and with it we curse men, who have been made in the likeness of God; 10from the same mouth come both blessing and cursing. My brethren, these things ought not be this way. 11Does a fountain send out from the same opening both fresh and bitter water?

RESTLESS is the Greek *akataschetos*, meaning "unsettled, undisciplined, unable to be restrained." [1]

PORE AND PARAPHRASE

PULL OUT

POSE

PLAN AND PIN

GROUP DISCUSSION
- *Can you think of a time when you were on the receiving end of an evil tongue? How did it feel?*
- *Discuss what the uses of poison reveal about the danger of an undisciplined tongue. How does it feel to know you have used your tongue as an instrument of poison?*

THE POWER OF WORDS IN OUR PERSONAL LIVES

Your words reveal the truth about your character

JAMES 1:19,26, AMP

[19]*Let every man be quick to hear [a ready listener], slow to speak, slow to take offense and to get angry.*

[26]*If anyone thinks himself to be religious (piously observant of the external duties of his faith) and does not bridle his tongue but deludes his own heart, this person's religious service is worthless (futile, barren).*

PORE AND PARAPHRASE

Listen first - let other person completely finish before speaking - think carefully about whether something really upsets you - and literally being angry -

PULL OUT

POSE

Try to not be overly sensitive -

PLAN AND PIN

- really listen to what is being said and was it meant to cause upset?

Jesus to the Pharisees

MATTHEW 12:34-36, AMP

³⁴Your offspring of vipers! How can you speak good things when you are evil (wicked)? For out of the fullness (the overflow, the superabundance) of the heart the mouth speaks.

³⁵The good man from his inner good treasure flings forth good things, and the evil man out of his inner evil storehouse flings forth evil things.

³⁶But I tell you, on the day of judgment men will have to give account for every idle (inoperative, nonworking) word they speak.

PORE AND PARAPHRASE

PULL OUT

POSE

PLAN AND PIN

The words of a wise man's mouth win him favor, but the lips of a fool consume him. Ecclesiastes 10:12, ESV

Your words have influence in your life

1 SAMUEL 30:1-6

¹Then it happened when David and his men came to Ziklag on the third day, that the Amalekites had made a raid on the Negev and on Ziklag, and had overthrown Ziklag and burned it with fire; ²and they took captive the women and all who were in it, both small and great, without killing anyone, and carried them off and went their way. ³When David and his men came to the city, behold, it was burned with fire, and their wives and their sons and their daughters had been taken captive. ⁴Then David and the people who were with him lifted their voices and wept until there was no strength in them to weep. ⁵Now David's two wives had been taken captive, Ahinoam the Jezreelitess and Abigail the widow of Nabal the Carmelite. ⁶Moreover David was greatly distressed because the people spoke of stoning him, for all the people were embittered, each one because of his sons and his daughters. But David strengthened himself in the LORD his God.

PORE AND PARAPHRASE

GROUP DISCUSSION
- *What do your words reveal about what is hidden in your heart?*
- *What kinds of things are you allowing to influence your heart and thought life?*

David speaking to himself in times of deep despair:
"Why are you in despair, O my soul? And why have you become disturbed within me? Hope in God, for I shall again praise Him." Psalm 42:5

PULL OUT

POSE

PLAN AND PIN

What are some specific things I am despairing about right now? Am I depending on others to encourage me or am I taking personal responsibility to strengthen myself in the Lord? What words can I choose to use to begin to speak "life" into this situation?

More Conversation Starters

Psalm 15:1-5; 37:30; 120:2-3; 139:1-4; Proverbs 21:23; 26:28; Philippians 2:14-16.

THE POWER OF WORDS IN OUR FAMILY

Your words and your children

DEUTERONOMY 6:6-8

⁶These words, which I am commanding you today, shall be on your heart. ⁷You shall teach them diligently to your sons and shall talk of them when you sit in your house and when you walk by the way and when you lie down and when you rise up. ⁸You shall bind them as a sign on your hand and they shall be as frontals on your forehead.

PORE AND PARAPHRASE

PULL OUT

POSE

PLAN AND PIN

Death and life are in the power of the tongue, and those who love it will eat its fruit. Proverbs 18:21

Your words and your spouse

1 PETER 3:1-2, ESV

¹Likewise, wives, be subject to your own husbands, so that even if some do not obey the word, they may be won without a word by the conduct of their wives, ²when they see your respectful and pure conduct.

PORE AND PARAPHRASE

PULL OUT

POSE

PLAN AND PIN

How difficult is it for me to *not say* anything? What current marital situation am I facing in which *not speaking* will have greater influence than any words I could say?

EPHESIANS 5:33

Nevertheless, each individual among you also is to love his own wife even as himself, and the wife must see to it that she respects her husband.

PORE AND PARAPHRASE

PULL OUT

POSE

PLAN AND PIN

Do I use a language of honor (terms and tone of respect) when addressing my spouse?

GROUP DISCUSSION
- *Sometimes it seems we speak more harshly to our spouses and children than we would to anyone else we know. Why? Do you recognize this in your life?*
- *Discuss some specific words you can use that will edify your husbands.*

JAMES 3:8-11

[8]No one can tame the tongue; it is a restless evil and full of deadly poison. [9]With it we bless our Lord and Father, and with it we curse men, who have been made in the likeness of God; [10]from the same mouth come both blessing and cursing. My brethren, these things ought not be this way. [11]Does a fountain send out from the same opening both fresh and bitter water?

PORE AND PARAPHRASE

PULL OUT

POSE

PLAN AND PIN

Does my mouth hold blessings or cursing regarding my husband? When he is around? When he is not around?

More Conversation Starters

Proverbs 12:25; 16:24; 19:13; 21:19; 31:26-28; Ephesians 6:4; Titus 2:3-4.

THE POWER OF WORDS IN OUR FRIENDSHIPS

Our words should provide encouragement and solace

Said of Job, whom God called "righteous"

JOB 4:3-4, ESV
³*Behold, you have instructed many,*
and you have strengthened the weak hands.
⁴*Your words have upheld him who was stumbling,*
and you have made firm the feeble knees.

For the despairing man there should be kindness from his friends;
so that he does not forsake the fear of the Almighty. **Job 6:14**

PORE AND PARAPHRASE

PULL OUT

POSE

PLAN AND PIN

Job's plea to his friends during his darkest hour

JOB 16:2-5, HCSB

²I have heard many things like these.
    You are all miserable comforters.
³Is there no end to your empty words?
    What provokes you that you continue testifying?
⁴If you were in my place I could also talk like you.
    I could string words together against you
        and shake my head at you, but I wouldn't.
⁵I would encourage you with my mouth,
    and the consolation from my lips would bring relief.

PORE AND PARAPHRASE

PULL OUT

POSE

PLAN AND PIN

Am I a trustworthy confidant for my friends? Am I a safe haven of encouragement and support?

Our words should build up and spur on to spiritual maturity

EPHESIANS 4:29-32, AMP

²⁹Let no foul or polluted language, nor evil word nor unwholesome or worthless talk [ever] come out of your mouth, but only such [speech] as is good and beneficial to the spiritual progress of others, as is fitting to the need and the occasion, that it may be a blessing and give grace (God's favor) to those who hear it. ³⁰And do not grieve the Holy Spirit of God [do not offend or vex or sadden Him], by Whom you were sealed (marked, branded as God's own, secured) for the day of redemption (of final deliverance through Christ from evil and the consequences of sin). ³¹Let all bitterness and indignation and wrath (passion, rage, bad temper) and resentment (anger, animosity) and quarreling (brawling, clamor, contention) and slander (evil-speaking, abusive or blasphemous language) be banished from you, with all malice (spite, ill will or baseness of any kind). ³²And become useful and helpful and kind to one another, tenderhearted (compassionate, understanding, loving-hearted), forgiving one another [readily and freely], as God in Christ forgave you.

> Oil and perfume make the heart glad, so a man's
> counsel is sweet to his friend. Proverbs 27:9

GROUP DISCUSSION

- *Ask an honest friend to answer these questions about you: Am I a positive and encouraging friend? Do you feel comfortable coming to me for advice?*
- *How can we consciously use our words to encourage friends?*

PORE AND PARAPHRASE

PULL OUT

POSE

PLAN AND PIN

Are my friendships only filled with superficial conversation or are they filled with purposeful attempts to bless, forgive, give grace, and express kindness, understanding, and forgiveness? How can I direct a conversation today toward spiritual things?

More Conversation Starters
Psalm 50:19-21; Proverbs 15:2-4; Jeremiah 9:7-9; 2 Timothy 2:16.23; James 5:9,13-15; 1 Peter 3:8-12; 4:9.

THE POWER OF WORDS IN OUR RELATIONSHIP WITH GOD

PSALM 103:1-6, AMP

¹Bless (affectionately, gratefully praise) the Lord, O my soul; and all that is [deepest] within me, bless His holy name!

²Bless (affectionately, gratefully praise) the Lord, O my soul, and forget not [one of] all His benefits—

³Who forgives [every one of] all your iniquities, Who heals [each one of] all your diseases,

⁴Who redeems your life from the pit and corruption, Who beautifies, dignifies, and crowns you with loving-kindness and tender mercy;

⁵Who satisfies your mouth [your necessity and desire at your personal age and situation] with good so that your youth, renewed, is like the eagle's [strong, overcoming, soaring]!

⁶The Lord executes righteousness and justice [not for me only, but] for all who are oppressed.

PORE AND PARAPHRASE

PULL OUT

POSE

PLAN AND PIN

Do I purposefully turn my attention to the things the Lord has done for me and engage in concentrated times of affectionate, grateful praise to Him? How can I remind myself of His benefits throughout the day and take time to bless Him for them?

HEBREWS 13:15-16

[15]Through Him [Jesus] then let us continually offer up a sacrifice of praise to God, that is, the fruit of lips that give thanks to His name. [16]And do not neglect doing good and sharing, for with such sacrifices God is pleased.

PORE AND PARAPHRASE

PULL OUT

POSE

PLAN AND PIN

What circumstance am I facing right now in which it is the most difficult for me to offer God praise? Stop now and find something in that situation to make the sacrifice of praise.

The Lord speaking of His chosen people

ISAIAH 29:13-14, HCSB

¹³*The Lord said:*
Because these people approach Me with their mouths
to honor Me with lip-service—
yet their hearts are far from Me,
and their worship consists of man-made rules
learned by rote—
¹⁴*therefore I will again confound these people*
with wonder after wonder.
The wisdom of their wise men will vanish,
and the understanding of the perceptive will be hidden.

PORE AND PARAPHRASE

PULL OUT

POSE

PLAN AND PIN

More Conversation Starters

Psalm 12:3-4; 34:1-3; 71:24; 119:171-172; 145:1-2; Isaiah 50:4-5; Philippians 4:4;
1 Thessalonians 5:16-18.

Summarize your conversation with God this week. In what specific ways have you been challenged to yield your tongue to the Lord's control? What steps can you take immediately to obey? What has been the most meaningful day of conversation have you had this week? Why? What verse has stirred the deepest conversation?

GROUP DISCUSSION

- *How can speaking praise to God even when we don't feel especially praiseful change our hearts?*
- *What is the power in speaking God's Word out loud?*

LIFE: THE EDITED VERSION

FATHER, Thank You for creating me to be a masterpiece to display Your glory. I believe that *Your* version of my life story is the best way to do that. This week I want to talk to You about the life that I have lived to this point and the life I will live from this day forward. I admit that it might be painful to release my own mapped-out plans to embrace Yours, but I desire deeply for my life to be Your edited version. As I consider the major goals, plans, and desires I have for my life, I've found that these are the things I've written into the story of my life:

Starting today, I give my life story to You. I want You to open my spiritual ears to hear what You want to tell me about these things. Help me to gracefully and gratefully accept what You will require me as You, the Divine Editor, rework my story. I am willing to adapt the details of my life to suit Your plan and purposes since I believe they are best for me.

Give me the courage to delete the things, desires, or even people that are infringing on Your perfect design for the book You are writing with my life. Allow me the grace to be completely content with what You've intended, no matter how different it is from my original plan. Lord, I trust You.

In Jesus' name, **AMEN.**

We are God's masterpiece. He has created us anew in Christ Jesus, so we can do the good things he planned for us long ago. **Ephesians 2:10, NLT**

DAY ONE
LIFE: THE EDITED VERSION

The vessel that he was making of clay was spoiled in the hand of the potter; so he remade it into another vessel, as it pleased the potter to make. Jeremiah 18:4

I'd like to be a great writer one day. It is one of my goals. For now, I remain in desperate need of an editor. Not just the kind who changes a grammatical error or two but one with patience to take my scrambled thoughts and make them palatable for the reader.

The editor. He takes the work that I've done and scans it closely. His job is not just to clean up any messes I made and was too tired to notice; he also spots unnecessary words, phrases, and (gulp) paragraphs. He cuts, shaves, dices, and carves until only what clearly communicates remains. The editor is the writer's friend and foe, partner and nemesis, comrade and enemy. The relationship is filled with bittersweet mountains and valleys as the two tramp together to the desired end. I know this unpredictable rapport all too well.

The initial stage of my writing project includes a meeting with my editor; it's the "honeymoon phase." I'm all starry-eyed and choose to entrust him with the finished product of my writing. Upon reviewing other resources he has helped to make successful, I agree that his judgment in the editorial process is trustworthy. We enter amicably into a partnership in which I trust him to make the final product of my book seamless and brilliant.

I spend weeks and months researching and putting pen to paper. I do my best to record truths that will touch the reader's heart and bring the biblical text to life. When I send in the final manuscript I breathe a sigh of relief as I excitedly wait to hear my editor's response. I anticipate that he will be just as pleased as I. Dreamily I imagine how he looks at my prose and nods approvingly. He celebrates my writing ability and praises me for all the work I have saved him.

I've been shaken awake from that "happily-ever-after" story one too many times. After five books and three Bible studies, I've not once had this become my reality.

Inevitably, the editor, once my friend, says to me three words guaranteed to deflate my honeymoon afterglow: "It's too long."

He begins to reformat the text, cutting unnecessary verbiage (that I spent hours thumbing through the thesaurus trying to craft) until the book reaches a more suitable length. When I see the edited version, I am appalled. I can't believe he has tossed away so much of my work. To me, everything was important! In fact, most of what he discarded I considered most important.

A quick glance over each page brings renewed disgust as I grasp the full extent of what he has done. My masterpiece has been destroyed. All of the good stuff has been taken out. A phone call crescendos into a waterfall of my opinions poured out on his desk. Calmly he listens and then explains with the authority of one who has mastered his job: "If the manuscript is too long, the reader will abandon you. Cutting it will add to its value. Trust me. I know what I'm doing."

Trust him? I don't even like him anymore.

Hesitantly, I submit.

The Divine Editor. He scans the works of life we have written. He looks not only for errors to blot out with the eraser of grace but also for unnecessary additions that must go. He knows the edited version of life will be most useful. So He cuts, shaves, dices, and carves until only that which will clearly communicate divine purpose remains.

We've spent years determining how our lives will look. Our design embraces desires and plans to ensure our happiness. We've composed our narratives—complete with a storybook ending. Carefully we craft details of education, family, friends, finances, and ministry involvement. With completed research we send the final manuscript to the Editor. We don't really want His advice—just approval and blessing.

We've met the Editor before. We even agree that He is trustworthy. We've seen His work on other life-projects and have been pleased with the results. We expect Him to see the wisdom of our plans, sit back in His editorial seat, nod in approval, and send back our manuscript with little more than one or two corrections. That's the honeymoon.

Yet the edited manuscript returns to us and we stand shocked as we glare at the seeming mess He has made. From start to finish nothing looks the same. The title has been changed. He calls it *Life: The Edited Version.* This new, shortened take on the topic of our existence doesn't in any way resemble what we originally turned in. From all initial glances, our book has been ruined.

The shock doesn't set in fully until we start reviewing the details chapter by chapter. The one we wrote on relationships now suggests cutting away many associations we thought necessary to our fulfillment. The busy, crammed schedule of ministry activity has been replaced by solitude, stillness, and silence. The plans for finances and family stand revamped.

The Editor's rewritten text shows our loved ones can be comfortable with far less extravagance than we anticipated. In fact, most of the themes of our chapters have been completely changed. His priorities have now been written in. We find inconsistencies with what we had in mind for almost every portion of our life story. We argue and debate heatedly. We seek to rebel against the work of the Expert, but we hear the calming voice of One having authority say, "If the manuscript is too full, it will lose its usefulness. You cannot do a thousand things well. Trust Me. I know what I'm doing."

He cuts. We frown. He deletes. We squirm. He molds. We object.

Finally ... hesitantly ... we trust and submit.

The book of our life is printed, bound, and duplicated for others to read. We are amazed at the results. We never knew that less could really amount to so much more.

I'm becoming a better writer, but I suspect I'll never be the greatest. I admit, my heart skips a beat when my editor sees something I've written and says, "You've done good, kid!"

I'm getting better at living, but my life's work is continually in progress. My Editor says if I keep trusting Him, He will show me where to make the right adjustments. I admit, my heart skips a beat at the thought of seeing Him one day, presenting Him my life's work, and hearing Him whisper, "Well done!"

THIS WEEK, HAVE A CONVERSATION WITH GOD.

Is my life God's version or mine? What are God's priorities for me in this season of my life? Am I devoted to those? What must I get rid of in my life to focus on God's goals for me?

GROUP DISCUSSION
- *What sort of things do you think God wants to delete from a Christian's life?*
- *What makes you nervous or fearful when you think about how God might edit your life?*

JEREMIAH 18:3-6, HCSB

³So I went down to the potter's house, and there he was, working away at the wheel. ⁴But the jar that he was making from the clay became flawed in the potter's hand, so he made it into another jar, as it seemed right for him to do.

⁵The word of the LORD came to me: ⁶"House of Israel, can I not treat you as this potter treats his clay?"—this is the LORD's declaration. "Just like clay in the potter's hand, so are you in My hand, house of Israel."

PORE AND PARAPHRASE

PULL OUT

POSE

PLAN AND PIN

RE-ORGANIZING OUR PRIORITIES

God's priorities versus our priorities

Concerning the Jews who had ignored God's priorities to pursue their own

HAGGAI 1:2-11, HCSB

²*"The LORD of Hosts says this: These people say: The time has not come for the house of the LORD to be rebuilt."*

³*The word of the LORD came through Haggai the prophet:* ⁴*"Is it a time for you yourselves to live in your paneled houses, while this house lies in ruins?"*

⁵*Now, the LORD of Hosts says this: "Think carefully about your ways:*

⁶*You have planted*
much but harvested little.
You eat
but never have enough to be satisfied.
You drink
but never have enough to become drunk.
You put on clothes
but never have enough to get warm.
The wage earner puts his wages
into a bag with a hole in it."

⁷*The LORD of Hosts says this: "Think carefully about your ways.* ⁸*Go up into the hills, bring down lumber, and build the house. Then I will be pleased with it and be glorified," says the LORD.* ⁹*"You expected much, but then it amounted to little. When you brought the harvest to your house, I ruined it. Why?" This is the declaration of the LORD of Hosts. "Because My house still lies in ruins, while each of you is busy with his own house.*

¹⁰*So on your account,*
the skies have withheld the dew
and the land its crops.

"I have summoned a drought
on the fields and the hills,
on the grain, new wine, olive oil,
and whatever the ground yields,
on the people and animals,
and on all that your hands produce."

"I came down from heaven not to follow my own whim but to accomplish the will of the One who sent me." John 6:38, MSG

PORE AND PARAPHRASE

PULL OUT

POSE

PLAN AND PIN

Does God's statement shock you: *"You brought the harvest to your house, I ruined it"*? In what ways has God's house (His priorities) lay in ruins in my life? Why have I procrastinated in pursuing God's priorities? What have I done instead of pursuing God's purposes? What consequences have I faced as a result?

God's word to those choosing to pursue His purpose in rebuilding His temple

HAGGAI 2:9, HCSB

"The final glory of this house will be greater than the first," says the LORD of Hosts. "I will provide peace in this place"—the declaration of the LORD of Hosts.

PORE AND PARAPHRASE

PULL OUT

POSE

PLAN AND PIN

GROUP DISCUSSION

- *Has God asked you to do something that didn't make sense? If so, what?*
- *Is there a "temple" in your life you've neglected for your own interests?*

LUKE 5:4-6,8-10, ESV

⁴When he had finished speaking, he said to Simon, "Put out into the deep and let down your nets for a catch." ⁵And Simon answered, "Master, we toiled all night and took nothing! But at your word I will let down the nets." ⁶And when they had done this, they enclosed a large number of fish, and their nets were breaking. ⁸But when Simon Peter saw it, he fell down at Jesus' knees, saying, "Depart from me, for I am a sinful man, O Lord." ⁹For he and all who were with him were astonished at the catch of fish that they had taken, ¹⁰and so also were James and John, sons of Zebedee, who were partners with Simon. And Jesus said to Simon, "Do not be afraid; from now on you will be catching men."

PORE AND PARAPHRASE

PULL OUT

POSE

PLAN AND PIN

When my hard efforts seem to be achieving no results, do I depend on my own skills and expertise rather than listen to God's direction? In what ways? When has God's way proven more efficient?

More Conversation Starters

1 Samuel 13:8-14; Proverbs 16:2-3; John 5:19; 1 Corinthians 2:2.

DAY THREE
GOD'S EDITED VERSION OF OUR SPIRITUAL LIVES

Getting rid of busyness

MARK 6:30-32

³⁰*The apostles gathered together with Jesus; and they reported to Him all that they had done and taught.* ³¹*And He said to them, "Come away by yourselves to a secluded place and rest a while." (For there were many people coming and going, and they did not even have time to eat.)* ³²*They went away in the boat to a secluded place by themselves.*

PORE AND PARAPHRASE

PULL OUT

POSE

PLAN AND PIN

In what ways have I taken on the church's exhausting infatuation with busyness and activity? Am I too busy to take care of even my most basic needs? the needs of my family?

MATTHEW 11:28-30

[28]*"Come to Me, all who are weary and heavy-laden, and I will give you rest.*
[29]*Take My yoke upon you and learn from Me, for I am gentle and humble
in heart, and YOU WILL FIND REST FOR YOUR SOULS.* [30]*For My yoke is easy and
My burden is light."*

PORE AND PARAPHRASE

PULL OUT

POSE

PLAN AND PIN

Right now, do I feel burdened by the "yoke" of religious rules and expectations?
Have they been imposed by others? by myself?

> **REST** is the Greek word *anapauo*, meaning "cessation,
> quiet, rest, silence, pause, or peacefulness." [1]

GROUP DISCUSSION
- *What are the benefits and differences
  between group Bible study and your own
  personal time with the Lord?*
- *What activities could you "edit out" of
  your schedule to make room for God?*

Immediately after the miracle of feeding the 5,000

MATTHEW 14:22-23, AMP

²²Then He directed the disciples to get into the boat and go before Him to the other side, while He sent away the crowds.

²³And after He had dismissed the multitudes, He went up into the hills by Himself to pray. When it was evening, He was still there alone.

PORE AND PARAPHRASE

PULL OUT

POSE

PLAN AND PIN

Do I value times of silence and solitude as much as the times I am busy and active? Do I feel guilty for taking time to be alone and recuperate?

Being spiritual isn't enough

REVELATION 2:2-4, ESV

[2]*"I know your works, your toil and your patient endurance, and how you cannot bear with those who are evil, but have tested those who call themselves apostles and are not, and found them to be false.* [3]*I know you are enduring patiently and bearing up for my name's sake, and you have not grown weary.* [4]*But I have this against you, that you have abandoned the love you had at first."*

The Greek word for **FIRST** here is *protos*, meaning "the first in time of place of any succession of things or people, first in rank." [2]

PORE AND PARAPHRASE

PULL OUT

POSE

PLAN AND PIN

Thinking back to the passion I felt for the Lord when I was first saved, has that "first love" been abandoned for other interests? What words describe the feelings I had when I was first saved?

More Conversation Starters
Psalm 23:1-3; 27:4; 37:7; 46:10; Jeremiah 2:2-3; Matthew 6:31-33; Mark 1:32-38; Luke 10:38-42; 1 Corinthians 13:1-8.

GOD'S EDITED VERSION OF OUR FINANCES

Jesus teaching the disciples

LUKE 16:19-25

[19]*"Now there was a rich man, and he habitually dressed in purple and fine linen, joyously living in splendor every day.* [20]*And a poor man named Lazarus was laid at his gate, covered with sores,* [21]*and longing to be fed with the crumbs which were falling from the rich man's table; besides, even the dogs were coming and licking his sores.* [22]*Now the poor man died and was carried away by the angels to Abraham's bosom; and the rich man also died and was buried.* [23]*In Hades he lifted up his eyes, being in torment, and saw Abraham far away and Lazarus in his bosom.* [24]*And he cried out and said, 'Father Abraham, have mercy on me, and send Lazarus so that he may dip the tip of his finger in water and cool off my tongue, for I am in agony in this flame.'* [25]*But Abraham said, 'Child, remember that during your life you received your good things, and likewise Lazarus bad things; but now he is being comforted here, and you are in agony.'"*

He who loves money will not be satisfied with money, nor he who loves abundance with its income. This too is vanity. When good things increase, those who consume them increase. So what is the advantage to their owners except to look on? **Ecclesiastes 5:10-11**

> Bring your full tithe to the Temple treasury so there will be ample provisions in my Temple. Test me in this and see if I don't open up heaven itself to you and pour out blessings beyond your wildest dreams. Malachi 3:10, MSG

PORE AND PARAPHRASE

PULL OUT

POSE

PLAN AND PIN

Am I trusting in earthly wealth to guarantee salvation? gain approval from God? secure status in my church or ministry?

Giving back to God

The Lord's message to His chosen people concerning tithing

LEVITICUS 27:30,32, NLT

³⁰One tenth of the produce of the land, whether grain from the fields or fruit from the trees, belongs to the LORD and must be set apart to him as holy.
³²Count off every tenth animal from your herds and flocks and set them apart for the LORD as holy.

CONTENTMENT is *autarkeia* in the original language, meaning "an inward self-sufficiency, as opposed to the lack or the desire of outward things." [3]

PORE AND PARAPHRASE

PULL OUT

POSE

PLAN AND PIN

1 TIMOTHY 6:6-10

⁶But godliness actually is a means of great gain when accompanied by contentment. ⁷For we have brought nothing into the world, so we cannot take anything out of it either. ⁸If we have food and covering, with these we shall be content. ⁹But those who want to get rich fall into temptation and a snare and many foolish and harmful desires which plunge men into ruin and destruction. ¹⁰For the love of money is a root of all sorts of evil, and some by longing for it have wandered away from the faith and pierced themselves with many griefs.

PORE AND PARAPHRASE

PULL OUT

POSE

PLAN AND PIN

Am I content with what I have right now? What does my relationship with money teach my loved ones about contentment?

More Conversation Starters

Proverbs 3:9; Matthew 6:21; 19:16-24; Mark 12:41-44; Luke 3:13-14; 2 Corinthians 9:7.

GOD'S EDITED VERSION OF OUR RELATIONSHIPS

Relationships with unbelievers

Paul's words to the believers at Corinth requesting they exercise discernment in their friendships and associations:

Do not be deceived: "Bad company corrupts good morals." 1 Corinthians 15:33

2 CORINTHIANS 6:14–17, NLT

¹⁴*Don't team up with those who are unbelievers. How can righteousness be a partner with wickedness? How can light live with darkness?* ¹⁵*What harmony can there be between Christ and the devil? How can a believer be a partner with an unbeliever?*

¹⁶*And what union can there be between God's temple and idols? For we are the temple of the living God. As God said:*

"I will live in them
    and walk among them.
I will be their God,
    and they will be my people.
¹⁷Therefore, come out from among unbelievers,
    and separate yourselves from them, says the LORD.
Don't touch their filthy things,
    and I will welcome you.

PORE AND PARAPHRASE

PULL OUT

POSE

PLAN AND PIN

Do I think carefully before entering intimate friendships and business partnerships?

The word HARMONY is translated "concord" in the KJV; the Greek word gives us our English word *symphony*. What type of chaos would erupt in a symphony if there were no union and harmony, if each musician played by his own tune?

As the Jews began the process of building the temple of the Lord

EZRA 4:1-3

¹*Now when the enemies of Judah and Benjamin heard that the people of the exile were building a temple to the LORD God of Israel, ²they approached Zerubbabel and the heads of fathers' households, and said to them, "Let us build with you, for we, like you, seek your God; and we have been sacrificing to Him since the days of Esarhaddon king of Assyria, who brought us up here." ³But Zerubbabel and Jeshua and the rest of the heads of fathers' households of Israel said to them, "You have nothing in common with us in building a house to our God; but we ourselves will together build to the LORD God of Israel, as King Cyrus, the king of Persia has commanded us."*

PORE AND PARAPHRASE

PULL OUT

POSE

PLAN AND PIN

Do the people with whom I associate have a beneficial or adverse affect on my success in pursuing God's purposes for me?

Friendship with believers

1 SAMUEL 18:1-4, NLT

¹*After David had finished talking with Saul, he met Jonathan, the king's son. There was an immediate bond between them, for Jonathan loved David.* ²*From that day on Saul kept David with him and wouldn't let him return home.* ³*And Jonathan made a solemn pact with David, because he loved him as he loved himself.* ⁴*Jonathan sealed the pact by taking off his robe and giving it to David, together with his tunic, sword, bow, and belt.*

PORE AND PARAPHRASE

PULL OUT

POSE

PLAN AND PIN

What deep friendships do I have, treasure, and remain loyal to? How have I shown this loyalty?

More Conversation Starters
Proverbs 13:20; 17:17; 18:24; 27:6,9-10,17; Ecclesiastes 4:9-12; 1 Corinthians 5:1-7; Ephesians 5:16-17; 2 Thessalonians 3:6-14; 2 Timothy 2:16-18.

Summarize your conversation with God this week. How have you been challenged to edit your life to conform to God's version? What steps can you take immediately to obey? What has been the most meaningful day of conversation have you had this week? Why? What verse has stirred the deepest conversation?

GROUP DISCUSSION
- *Why is it crucial to be careful about who is included in your intimate circle of friends?*
- *How can having relationships with non-Christians affect our lives, for good and for bad? Is there a place for them?*

WHO IS THE LORD?

LORD, Keep me away from the things that slowly take Your place in my heart. Although I am trying to keep my attention solely focused on You as the only One worthy of my adoration, I admit that I often succumb to the lure of earthly gods. I begin trusting people, places, and things when I am to trust only You. I don't want to give in to the worldly perspectives that lead to a life of idolatry. Will You please place Your fiery hedge of protection around my heart so that it does not long for any false god? This week, clearly reveal everything and everyone that I have knowingly or unknowingly given the place that should be reserved for only You.

Speak clearly, Lord; I'm listening and I want to be cleansed so that I might serve You more fully.

In the only worthy name, the name of Jesus, **AMEN.**

We know that the Son of God has come, and he has given us understanding so that we can know the true God. And now we live in fellowship with the true God because we live in fellowship with his Son, Jesus Christ. He is the only true God, and he is eternal life. Dear children, keep away from anything that might take God's place in your hearts. **1 John 5:20-22, NLT**

WHO IS THE LORD?

Jackson was celebrating his fourth birthday. Excited at the prospect of a fun-filled day, he dressed quickly for church on that Sunday morning. I fitted him with a birthday hat and secured a dollar bill to his shirt. I knew that the dollar bill and hat would tip people off to the importance of the day and encourage them to assist me in celebrating. By the end of the church service my little man had almost $30 attached to his sweater.

Seizing the opportunity, I thought it was only fitting that Jackson learn a lesson in tithing. I explained to him that in obedience and thanksgiving we must always give the first portion to the Lord from the resources that He gives to us. I ask him to choose a few dollars that we could give to God. He carefully selected several. I took his hand to guide him from the sanctuary into the lobby where the church keeps an offering container. As we emerged from the sanctuary, I felt Jackson's hand go limp and noticed his eyes widen with emotion. He scanned the lobby anxiously. "Jackson," I asked, "What's wrong? What are you looking for?" Without hesitation he responded in childlike simplicity, "Didn't you say we were bringing money to the Lord? Is He here in the lobby somewhere?"

I laughed and tried to explain the finer points of giving an offering to God as we walked toward the tithing container.

My explanation was cut short when Jackson gasped and stopped dead in his tracks. Looking across the lobby, his eyes met with the man who leads praise and worship during our services. With an outgoing personality, this man who holds the microphone on stage each week seemed larger than life to my small child. Eyes agape and mouth widened, Jackson exclaimed, "Mom, is that THE LORD?"

The writer posed a similar question in Psalm 24. "Who is this King of glory?" His simple yet often forgotten response must resonate in the hearts of everyone on the earth, "The LORD strong and mighty, the LORD mighty in battle" (v. 8). He alone is the Lord.

With widened eyes and mouths agape like seeking children, we point at the human celebrities of our faith and set them on a pedestal next to God. Their positions in our hearts become so parallel that we have trouble distinguishing them from the Savior of our souls.

We read their commentaries on the Bible more than the Bible itself. We rush to a meeting to hear from them instead of a personal one-on-one meeting with God. When they minister, we applaud in their faces instead of at His feet. We have unashamedly dished out adoration reserved for the Most High.

How often have you—have I—subconsciously placed mere humans in the position intended only for the Holy One? The more visible the gift and the more celebrated the ministry, the more we subconsciously align a human with the Almighty. It is alarming how frequently the church has glorified the ones for whom Christ died. We have begun to appoint and worship our "heroes." Strangely enough, the greatest of these are most often the ones for whom Christ has given the most mercy and extended the deepest deliverance. Friend, I can attest to that.

Our tendency to place others in the position reserved for God must end. We must turn our gaze and attention to the Lord alone. He alone deserves our utmost respect and celebration. When we sing, we do so to the glory of the Lord. When we serve, we do so out of reverence for the Lord. When we give, we do so out of the abundance He has allowed. In all these things—in our eating and drinking and playing and working—our object of affection and passion must be clearly pinpointed. We must not allow the veil of humanity to stand in the way of our clear view of God.

No more heroes. No more Christian celebrities. Seek Him alone. He is the one worthy of your everything. Today, ask yourself, "Who is my lord?" and see where your search leads.

"Idolatry is not limited to the worship of false images, but it is placing anything or anyone before God as the object of allegiance and devotion." [1]

THIS WEEK, HAVE A CONVERSATION WITH GOD.

Do I have a tendency to cling to a particular person in my life? Who? Why? Who have I hired to be "Jesus" for me? Who do I need to "fire" from that position so that the Lord can take that seat of prominence in my life?

PSALM 24, ESV

¹The earth is the LORD's and the fullness thereof,
the world and those who dwell therein,
²for he has founded it upon the seas
and established it upon the rivers.
³Who shall ascend the hill of the LORD?
And who shall stand in his holy place?
⁴He who has clean hands and a pure heart,
who does not lift up his soul to what is false
and does not swear deceitfully.
⁵He will receive blessing from the LORD
and righteousness from the God of his salvation.
⁶Such is the generation of those who seek him,
who seek the face of the God of Jacob.
⁷Lift up your heads, O gates!
And be lifted up, O ancient doors,
that the King of glory may come in.
⁸Who is this King of glory?
The LORD, strong and mighty,
the LORD, mighty in battle!
⁹Lift up your heads, O gates!
And lift them up, O ancient doors,
that the King of glory may come in.
¹⁰Who is this King of glory?
The LORD of hosts,
he is the King of glory!

GROUP DISCUSSION

- *Are we guilty of creating Christian celebrities? How can we stop the process?*
- *How can we become like the person described in Psalm 24:4?*

PORE AND PARAPHRASE

PULL OUT

POSE

PLAN AND PIN

DAY TWO
HUMAN HEROES

EXODUS 32:1-4

¹Now when the people saw that Moses delayed to come down from the mountain, the people assembled about Aaron and said to him, "Come, make us a god who will go before us; as for this Moses, the man who brought us up from the land of Egypt, we do not know what has become of him."

²Aaron said to them, "Tear off the gold rings which are in the ears of your wives, your sons, and your daughters, and bring them to me." ³Then all the people tore off the gold rings which were in their ears and brought them to Aaron. ⁴He took this from their hand, and fashioned it with a graving tool and made it into a molten calf; and they said, "This is your god, O Israel, who brought you up from the land of Egypt."

PORE AND PARAPHRASE

PULL OUT

POSE

PLAN AND PIN

During seasons of waiting in my life, do I have a tendency to make another "god" from something I can interact with through my physical senses? How have I been disappointed when my expectations of others have been too high?

Response to idols

Paul's response to the audience's attempt to worship him and Barnabas

ACTS 14:8-15, NIV

[8]*In Lystra there sat a man crippled in his feet, who was lame from birth and had never walked.* [9]*He listened to Paul as he was speaking. Paul looked directly at him, saw that he had faith to be healed* [10]*and called out, "Stand up on your feet!" At that, the man jumped up and began to walk.*

[11]*When the crowd saw what Paul had done, they shouted in the Lycaonian language, "The gods have come down to us in human form!"*

[12]*Barnabas they called Zeus, and Paul they called Hermes because he was the chief speaker.* [13]*The priest of Zeus, whose temple was just outside the city, brought bulls and wreaths to the city gates because he and the crowd wanted to offer sacrifices to them.*

[14]*But when the apostles Barnabas and Paul heard of this, they tore their clothes and rushed out into the crowd, shouting:* [15]*"Men, why are you doing this? We too are only men, human like you. We are bringing you good news, telling you to turn from these worthless things to the living God, who made heaven and earth and sea and everything in them.*

PORE AND PARAPHRASE

PULL OUT

POSE

PLAN AND PIN

Do I have any tendency to worship the messengers of God's Word more than God Himself? Am I connected with any ministries or ministers that readily receive worship instead of diverting it to God?

DEUTERONOMY 4:16-19, NLT

16Do not corrupt yourselves by making an idol in any form—whether of a man or a woman, 17an animal on the ground, a bird in the sky, 18a small animal that scurries along the ground, or a fish in the deepest sea. 19And when you look up into the sky and see the sun, moon, and stars—all the forces of heaven—don't be seduced into worshiping them. The LORD your God gave them to all the peoples of the earth.

PORE AND PARAPHRASE

PULL OUT

POSE

PLAN AND PIN

GROUP DISCUSSION
- *If someone praised you as the people in Lystra praised Paul and Barnabas, how do you think you would respond?*
- *Do you know anyone who seems to worship nature rather than its Creator?*

Paul writing to warn the Colossian believers about false teachers

COLOSSIANS 2:18-19

[18]Let no one keep defrauding you of your prize by delighting in self-abasement and the worship of the angels, taking his stand on visions he has seen, inflated without cause by his fleshly mind,

[19]and not holding fast to the head, from whom the entire body, being supplied and held together by the joints and ligaments, grows with a growth which is from God.

PORE AND PARAPHRASE

PULL OUT

POSE

PLAN AND PIN

More Conversation Starters

Deuteronomy 12:29-31; Habakkuk 2:18-20; Matthew 4:8-10; Revelation 22:8-9.

SECRET IDOLATRY

The Lord to the prophet Ezekiel

EZEKIEL 8:9-12, ESV

⁹*He said to me, "Go in [to the temple], and see the vile abominations that they are committing here." ¹⁰So I went in and saw. And there, engraved on the wall all around, was every form of creeping things and loathsome beasts, and all the idols of the house of Israel. ¹¹And before them stood seventy men of the elders of the house of Israel ... Each had his censer in his hand, and the smoke of the cloud of incense went up. ¹²Then he said to me, "Son of man, have you seen what the elders of the house of Israel are doing in the dark, each in his room of pictures? For they say, 'The LORD does not see us, the LORD has forsaken the land.'"*

PORE AND PARAPHRASE

PULL OUT

POSE

PLAN AND PIN

The idols of Israel were in the temple. What idols (activities, people, ideologies) have I kept "in the dark," cloaked in a façade of "religion"?

PSALM 44:20-21, ESV

²⁰*If we had forgotten the name of our God
     or spread out our hands to a foreign god,*
²¹*would not God discover this?
     For he knows the secrets of the heart.*

The SPREADING OUT of hands was a posture used in times of heartfelt prayer.[2]

PORE AND PARAPHRASE

PULL OUT

POSE

PLAN AND PIN

God, please reveal to me the "secrets of my heart." Here are some of the ones I know of already:

Your god is what you seek. It's what you love, trust in,
worship, serve, and allow to control you.

COLOSSIANS 3:5, NLT

So put to death the sinful, earthly things lurking within you. Have nothing to do with sexual immorality, impurity, lust, and evil desires. Don't be greedy, for a greedy person is an idolater, worshiping the things of this world.

PORE AND PARAPHRASE

PULL OUT

POSE

PLAN AND PIN

What object or person do I have an insatiable desire for? What do I covet? How does this reveal the hidden idols of my heart?

GROUP DISCUSSION
- *Why do we think we can keep God in the dark about our idols?*
- *Have you recognized any idols in your life this week? If you are willing to share, please do so.*

1 JOHN 2:15-17, ESV

[15]*Do not love the world or the things in the world. If anyone loves the world, the love of the Father is not in him.* [16]*For all that is in the world—the desires of the flesh and the desires of the eyes and pride in possessions—is not from the Father but is from the world.* [17]*And the world is passing away along with its desires, but whoever does the will of God abides forever.*

PORE AND PARAPHRASE

PULL OUT

POSE

PLAN AND PIN

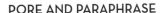

You shall love the LORD your God with all your heart and
with all your soul and with all your might. Deuteronomy 6:5

More Conversation Starters

Job 31:26-28; Psalm 16:4; Matthew 6:24; Mark 7:20-23; 12:29; Galatians 5:19-21; Ephesians 5:5.

CONSEQUENCES OF IDOLATRY

ROMANS 1:21-32, NLT

²¹Yes, they knew God, but they wouldn't worship him as God or even give him thanks. And they began to think up foolish ideas of what God was like. As a result, their minds became dark and confused. ²²Claiming to be wise, they instead became utter fools. ²³And instead of worshiping the glorious, ever-living God, they worshiped idols made to look like mere people and birds and animals and reptiles.

²⁴So God abandoned them to do whatever shameful things their hearts desired. As a result, they did vile and degrading things with each other's bodies. ²⁵They traded the truth about God for a lie. So they worshiped and served the things God created instead of the Creator himself, who is worthy of eternal praise! Amen.

²⁶That is why God abandoned them to their shameful desires. Even the women turned against the natural way to have sex and instead indulged in sex with each other. ²⁷And the men, instead of having normal sexual relations with women, burned with lust for each other. Men did shameful things with other men, and as a result of this sin, they suffered within themselves the penalty they deserved.

²⁸Since they thought it foolish to acknowledge God, he abandoned them to their foolish thinking and let them do things that should never be done. ²⁹Their lives became full of every kind of wickedness, sin, greed, hate, envy, murder, quarreling, deception, malicious behavior, and gossip. ³⁰They are backstabbers, haters of God, insolent, proud, and boastful. They invent new ways of sinning, and they disobey their parents. ³¹They refuse to understand, break their promises, are heartless, and have no mercy. ³²They know God's justice requires that those who do these things deserve to die, yet they do them anyway. Worse yet, they encourage others to do them, too.

PORE AND PARAPHRASE

PULL OUT

POSE

PLAN AND PIN

Consider the astounding windfall of ill effects suffered as a result of idolatry listed in this passage. Recall a time when placing someone or something in God's place in my life caused a windfall of consequences for me.

King Solomon's idolatrous reign in Israel affects his son

1 KINGS 11:9-12, ESV

⁹*The* LORD *was angry with Solomon, because his heart had turned away from the* LORD*, the God of Israel, who had appeared to him twice* ¹⁰*and had commanded him concerning this thing, that he should not go after other gods. But he did not keep what the* LORD *commanded.* ¹¹*Therefore the* LORD *said to Solomon, "Since this has been your practice and you have not kept my covenant and my statutes that I have commanded you, I will surely tear the kingdom from you and will give it to your servant.* ¹²*Yet for the sake of David your father I will not do it in your days, but I will tear it out of the hand of your son."*

PORE AND PARAPHRASE

PULL OUT

POSE

PLAN AND PIN

GROUP DISCUSSION
- *Share a time when idolatry had an ill effect on you or someone you love.*
- *Read 1 Samuel 15:23 (p. 69). When have you been guilty of rebellion and stubbornness? What are the similarities between rebellion and witchcraft?*

Samuel to King Saul, who acted rebelliously against God

1 SAMUEL 15:22-23, NLT

²²*Samuel replied, "What is more pleasing to the LORD : your burnt offerings and sacrifices or your obedience to his voice? Listen! Obedience is better than sacrifice, and submission is better than offering the fat of rams. ²³Rebellion is as sinful as witchcraft, and stubbornness as bad as worshiping idols. So because you have rejected the command of the LORD , he has rejected you as king."*

PORE AND PARAPHRASE

PULL OUT

POSE

PLAN AND PIN

Am I rebellious? Stubborn? In what ways? What gift from God might be withheld as a consequence of this? What American cultural practices do I think most heavily lure today's Christian away from full allegiance to God? Which of these practices have affected me?

More Conversation Starters

Deuteronomy 17:2-7; 27:15; 32:15-38; 1 Samuel 8:1-20; 2 Kings 10:28-32; 17:12-23; Psalm 66:18; 106:35-41; Ecclesiastes 12:14; Isaiah 1:11-17; 42:17; 45:16; Jeremiah 2:5-9,17; 5:19; Ezekiel 6:9-10; 14:2-6; Hosea 13:1-9; 1 Corinthians 10:19-22; 2 Corinthians 11:3; Acts 7:37-43; Titus 2:11-13.

BREAKING THE CYCLE

Young King Hezekiah, son of one of the most wicked and vile kings of Judah, Ahaz

2 KINGS 18:3-7, ESV

³*He did what was right in the eyes of the LORD, according to all that David his father had done. ⁴He removed the high places and broke the pillars and cut down the Asherah. And he broke in pieces the bronze serpent that Moses had made, for until those days the people of Israel had made offerings to it (it was called Nehushtan). ⁵He trusted in the LORD, the God of Israel, so that there was none like him among all the kings of Judah after him, nor among those who were before him. ⁶For he held fast to the LORD. He did not depart from following him, but kept the commandments that the LORD commanded Moses. ⁷And the LORD was with him; wherever he went out, he prospered. He rebelled against the king of Assyria and would not serve him.*

PORE AND PARAPHRASE

PULL OUT

POSE

PLAN AND PIN

Is there a legacy of idolatry in my life? What "pillars," "high places," and "Asherahs" is the Lord challenging me to boldly destroy in light of my heritage?

Challenging leaders

Daniel and his three friends' response when threatened with death as they refused to bow down and worship the gods of Babylon

DANIEL 3:16-18, HCSB

[16]*Shadrach, Meshach, and Abednego replied to the king, "Nebuchadnezzar, we don't need to give you an answer to this question.* [17]*If the God we serve exists, then He can rescue us from the furnace of blazing fire, and He can rescue us from the power of you, the king.* [18]*But even if He does not rescue us, we want you as king to know that we will not serve your gods or worship the gold statue you set up."*

PORE AND PARAPHRASE

PULL OUT

POSE

PLAN AND PIN

What are some consequences I may face (at work, at home, in the neighborhood, in an organization) if I choose not to acquiesce to their standards? Am I confident in God's ability to protect me when I go against the culture and stand firm?

Challenging your family

Asa, king of Israel for 41 years

1 KINGS 15:12-13

¹²He also put away the male cult prostitutes from the land and removed all the idols which his fathers had made.

¹³He also removed Maacah his [grand]mother from being queen mother, because she had made a horrid image as an Asherah; and Asa cut down her horrid image and burned it at the brook Kidron.

PORE AND PARAPHRASE

PULL OUT

POSE

PLAN AND PIN

What family members will I have to oppose to be devoted to the sole worship of God?

GROUP DISCUSSION
- *How do we break a cycle of idol worship?*
- *When is it appropriate to oppose your family on a matter of idols?*

Jacob's challenge to his family

GENESIS 35:1-4, HCSB

¹God said to Jacob, "Get up! Go to Bethel and settle there. Build an altar there to the God who appeared to you when you fled from your brother Esau."

²So Jacob said to his family and all who were with him, "Get rid of the foreign gods that are among you. Purify yourselves and change your clothes. ³We must get up and go to Bethel. I will build an altar there to the God who answered me in my day of distress. He has been with me everywhere I have gone."

⁴Then they gave Jacob all their foreign gods and their earrings, and Jacob hid them under the oak near Shechem.

PORE AND PARAPHRASE

PULL OUT

POSE

PLAN AND PIN

How can you challenge your family to move away from a life of idolatry? What can you do to set the example?

More Conversation Starters

Exodus 20:3-6; 23:13; Leviticus 19:4; Deuteronomy 9:11-21; 2 Kings 23:1-25; Psalm 51:17; 97:7; 119:36-37; Mark 12:29-30; John 4:23-24; 1 Corinthians 5:11; 10:14.

Summarize your conversation with God this week. What people, places, activities, or things have you allowed to take God's place in your life? What steps can you take immediately to respond? What has been the most meaningful day of conversation have you had this week? Why? What verse has stirred the deepest conversation?

THE **HEDGE** THAT PROTECTS

THANK YOU FATHER for being El-Rohi, God my Shepherd. Today, I admit my need for You to guide me, love me, protect me, and care for me as a shepherd does for his beloved sheep. Yet often I inadvertently put my confidence in temporal things to give me the security that really can only come from You. Sometimes, I have placed confidence in my financial status, career success, marital status, or earthly possessions to be a refuge from hurt and danger. But I have found those things to be lacking. Nothing and no one is truly trustworthy. My complete confidence must be in You and You alone—the only One who can truly take care of my body, soul, and spirit.

Father, I must admit, life has brought several hurtful circumstances into my life that have caused me to waver in my belief that You do have my best interests in mind. Some of these things are:

1.

2.

3.

Although I may never understand why You have allowed these things, I will choose to trust You. This week, will You speak to me, Lord? Remind me of Your desire and ability to protect me in spite of things that have happened or may happen in the future. Help me to trust in the tender care of Your sovereignty in my life. Reignite my confidence in You as my only true source of real protection. And as my confidence grows, I ask, Lord, that You will guard me and those I love with a hedge of your divine favor. Be my strong shield of defense. I trust You Lord, today and every day.

In the name of El-Rohi, my great guarding Shepherd, **AMEN.**

"If you'll hold on to me for dear life," says GOD, *"I'll get you out of any trouble. I'll give you the best of care if you'll only get to know and trust me. Call me and I'll answer, be at your side in bad times; I'll rescue you, then throw you a party. I'll give you a long life, give you a long drink of salvation!"* **Psalm 91:14-16,** MSG

DAY ONE
THE HEDGE THAT PROTECTS

Have You not made a hedge about him and his house and all that he has, on every side? Job 1:10

As long as I can remember I have visited my paternal grandparents each summer at their home in urban Baltimore. My parents and all of my siblings would drive from Texas to the very house where my father grew up. I have fond memories of lazy summer days spent sitting on the front porch of their row house, wiping the sweat from my brow while talking about life and sharing our stories. Crab feasts and trips to the Baltimore Harbor always sealed our time with them and became a part of our family tradition.

We have long desired for them to move closer to us, but they stubbornly insist on staying right where they have been for almost 50 years. We continue to ask them to reconsider because the neighborhood they once loved for its solace and serenity has changed. The cool ease of the 1950s has been trampled by a hip-hop urban community bringing an infestation of drug trafficking, loitering, and alcoholism. The once-thriving businesses that lined the streets are now closed and caged by thick bars covering the windows and wooden boards slathered with lewd graffiti. Every few moments a police car races by, bringing frowns to my tender grandparents' faces. Each siren brings a startling reminder of what their beloved neighborhood has become.

I clearly remember the time my entire family had to be quickly corralled off the front porch into the house when gunshots rang out nearby. And the occasion when my grandfather pointed to the street corner to show us a drug sale in progress. I even recall a time when a man was shot directly in front of their house during one of our visits.

I'm amazed that my grandparents choose to stay. From my perspective, an old, sweet married couple has no business in a neighborhood like that, but they have always given us the same reason for their refusal to leave. Their words, tempered with humility, still bring tears to my eyes: "God protects us here." The bullets fly but have never hit their home. Strange characters hang around on the street corners and even walk by the front porch, but they just look and leave. Police helicopters roar overhead, but their peace remains unscathed. In fact, in all the 50 years that Evelyn and Arthur Evans have lived in that same row house they have never even had a burglary, much less been directly affected by the war that wages right outside their doors. The two houses directly connected to theirs have seen the worst evil imaginable, but theirs has remained untouched.

Now, as an adult, I see my grandparents' home with new eyes. Although connected to the houses on either side, my grandparents' house seems strangely detached from the rest. A fiery wall of security is so evident it can almost be seen with the physical eye. God's divine hedge of protection surrounds every corner of their residence, creating a fortified shelter for those inside. It serves as a barrier between them and the world. Instead of turmoil and chaos, their home is filled to overflowing with refuge, peace, and solace. To be in their home is to be in the safest place in the world because they are protected, not by window bars and alarm systems, but by the mighty hedge placed around them by the God they faithfully and unashamedly serve. This hedge sustains, protects, and delivers. It guards, shields, and assures victory for those within its boundaries. It's been promised not only to my godly grandparents but also to all who seek refuge in Him.

> *The eternal God is your refuge, and underneath are the everlasting arms. He will drive out your enemy before you. Deuteronomy 33:27, NIV*
>
> *You are my hiding place; you will protect me from trouble and surround me with songs of deliverance. Psalm 32:7, NIV*
>
> *We may boldly say: The Lord is my helper; I will not be afraid. What can man do to me? Hebrews 13:6, HCSB*

The hedge that protects cannot be penetrated without permission from the God who placed it there. He is the keeper at its gate and it remains intact as long as He says so.

I have just returned to Texas from my yearly visit to my grandparents' home in Baltimore. We still had delicious Maryland steamed crabs, a visit to Baltimore's fabulous harbor, and a beautiful front porch where my grandparents, now a little slower and older, sit telling stories about what the Lord has done in their lives. But some things have changed. I don't go to Baltimore with my parents anymore. Now I take my children along. I meander on that porch, wiping the sweat from my brow, while watching my boys sit at the feet of their great-grandparents, who live each day under the hedge that protects.

THIS WEEK, HAVE A CONVERSATION WITH GOD.

Do I fear my surroundings more than I trust in the protection of God? Have I placed ultimate trust in anything or anyone other than God to protect me and my loved ones from harm? What has happened to me that I blame God for? Will I commit to trust in God's sovereignty in my circumstances?

PSALM 118:6

The LORD is for me, I will not fear;
What can man do to me?

PORE AND PARAPHRASE

PULL OUT

POSE

PLAN AND PIN

GROUP DISCUSSION
- *How have you experienced the hedge that protects?*
- *Why do so many Christians live in a spirit of fear?*

THE TRUSTWORTHY PROTECTION OF EL-ROHI

God protects even in times of hardship

David writing in celebration of Yahweh, his Shepherd

PSALM 23:4-5

⁴*Even though I walk through the valley of the shadow of death,*
I fear no evil, for You are with me;
Your rod and Your staff, they comfort me.
⁵*You prepare a table before me in the presence of my enemies;*
You have anointed my head with oil;
My cup overflows.

PORE AND PARAPHRASE

PULL OUT

POSE

PLAN AND PIN

PSALM 33:18-22, NLT

¹⁸*The LORD watches over those who fear him,*
those who rely on his unfailing love.
¹⁹*He rescues them from death*
and keeps them alive in times of famine.
²⁰*We put our hope in the LORD.*
He is our help and our shield.
²¹*In him our hearts rejoice,*
for we trust in his holy name.
²²*Let your unfailing love surround us, LORD,*
for our hope is in you alone.

PORE AND PARAPHRASE

PULL OUT

POSE

PLAN AND PIN

What have I put my hope (confident expectation) in for protection? Today, what do I need God to watch over me regarding?

GROUP DISCUSSION

- *Spend time praying for one another using the words of Psalm 23 and 33.*
- *Do you know someone personally whose life reflects God's hedge of protection?*

God uses unseen supernatural forces to provide protection

2 KINGS 6:14-17, NLT

¹⁴*One night the king of Aram sent a great army with many chariots and horses to surround the city. ¹⁵When the servant of the man [Elisha] of God got up early the next morning and went outside, there were troops, horses, and chariots everywhere.*

"Oh, sir, what will we do now?" the young man cried to Elisha.

¹⁶*"Don't be afraid!" Elisha told him. "For there are more on our side than on theirs!" ¹⁷Then Elisha prayed, "O LORD, open his eyes and let him see!" The LORD opened the young man's eyes, and when he looked up, he saw that the hillside around Elisha was filled with horses and chariots of fire.*

PORE AND PARAPHRASE

PULL OUT

POSE

PLAN AND PIN

What "great army" from the enemy's territory has made a surprise attack in my life recently? How does it appear that they outnumber the Lord's army on my side? Lord, please open my spiritual eyes to see Your power and protection with me.

ISAIAH 40:21-26, NLT

²¹*Haven't you heard? Don't you understand? Are you deaf to the words of God-the words he gave before the world began? Are you so ignorant?* ²²*God sits above the circle of the earth. The people below seem like grasshoppers to him! He spreads out the heavens like a curtain and makes his tent from them.* ²³*He judges the great people of the world and brings them all to nothing.* ²⁴*They hardly get started, barely taking root, when he blows on them and they wither. The wind carries them off like chaff.*

²⁵*"To whom will you compare me? Who is my equal?" asks the Holy One.*

²⁶*Look up into the heavens. Who created all the stars? He brings them out like an army, one after another, calling each by its name. Because of his great power and incomparable strength, not a single one is missing.*

PORE AND PARAPHRASE

PULL OUT

POSE

PLAN AND PIN

On a separate sheet of paper, make a list of the powerful characteristics of our God as listed in this passage. Use this list to build your faith in His ability to protect you.

MORE CONVERSATION STARTERS

Joshua 23:12-13; 1 Chronicles 5:20; Job 5:19-22; Psalm 18:2; 34:15; 62; 91:1-16; 128:1; Isaiah 25:9; 40:31; Romans 8:31; 1 John 5:4-5.

DAY THREE
FALSE SENSE OF SECURITY

The Lord's rebuke to the Jewish rulers who were seeking an alliance with Egypt

ISAIAH 30:1-5, NLT

[1]"What sorrow awaits my rebellious children," says the LORD. "You make plans that are contrary to mine. You make alliances not directed by my Spirit, thus piling up your sins. [2]For without consulting me, you have gone down to Egypt for help. You have put your trust in Pharaoh's protection. You have tried to hide in his shade. [3]But by trusting Pharaoh, you will be humiliated, and by depending on him, you will be disgraced. [4]For though his power extends to Zoan and his officials have arrived in Hanes, [5]all who trust in him will be ashamed. He will not help you. Instead, he will disgrace you."

"In this case forming an alliance is likened to weaving a garment." [1]

PORE AND PARAPHRASE

PULL OUT

POSE

PLAN AND PIN

Am I seeking security in something or someone other than God? What is the cost I am paying for my alliance with this thing/activity/person?

Security in self

The Lord's response to a human attempt to gain status and fulfill plans at the cost of obedience to Him

GENESIS 11:4-8, HCSB

⁴And they said, "Come, let us build ourselves a city and a tower with its top in the sky. Let us make a name for ourselves; otherwise, we will be scattered over the face of the whole earth."

⁵Then the LORD came down to look over the city and the tower that the men were building. ⁶The LORD said, "If, as one people all having the same language, they have begun to do this, then nothing they plan to do will be impossible for them. ⁷Come, let Us go down there and confuse their language so that they will not understand one another's speech." ⁸So the LORD scattered them from there over the face of the whole earth, and they stopped building the city.

PORE AND PARAPHRASE

PULL OUT

POSE

PLAN AND PIN

What circumstance am I in right now in which I am trusting in my own abilities more than God's? How might the Lord respond to my self-sufficiency?

Deliverance comes not from things which are created but from the Creator

1 SAMUEL 17:45-47, HCSB

[45]David said to the Philistine, "You come against me with a dagger, spear, and sword, but I come against you in the name of the LORD of Hosts, the God of Israel's armies—you have defied Him. [46]Today, the LORD will hand you over to me. Today, I'll strike you down, cut your head off, and give the corpses of the Philistine camp to the birds of the sky and the creatures of the earth. Then all the world will know that Israel has a God,[47]and this whole assembly will know that it is not by sword or by spear that the LORD saves, for the battle is the LORD's. He will hand you over to us."

For the weapons of our warfare are not of the flesh, but divinely powerful for the destruction of fortresses. 2 Corinthians 10:4

PORE AND PARAPHRASE

PULL OUT

POSE

PLAN AND PIN

GROUP DISCUSSION
- *What Babels do people build today?*
- *What things give false hope? In what might nonbelievers say they hope?*

PSALM 33:13-17, ESV

¹³The LORD looks down from heaven;
*   he sees all the children of man;*
¹⁴from where he sits enthroned he looks out
*   on all the inhabitants of the earth,*
¹⁵he who fashions the hearts of them all
*   and observes all their deeds.*
¹⁶The king is not saved by his great army;
*   a warrior is not delivered by his great strength.*
¹⁷The war horse is a false hope for salvation,
*   and by its great might it cannot rescue.*

FALSE HOPE translates *sheqer,* meaning "a lie, falsehood, delusion." [2]

PORE AND PARAPHRASE

PULL OUT

POSE

PLAN AND PIN

More Conversation Starters

Numbers 14:1-23; 1 Samuel 17:26, Psalm 20:7; Proverbs 18:10; Isaiah 30:1-7; Jeremiah 17:5-6; Daniel 6:6-28; Zechariah 2:5; 2 Corinthians 3:5; Philippians 4:13.

DAY FOUR
GOD'S PROTECTION WHEN I'M INTIMIDATED

When the tasks seems bigger than me ...

Yahweh to Jeremiah, who felt ill equipped for the assignment given to him

JEREMIAH 1:17-19, ESV

¹⁷"But you, dress yourself for work; arise, and say to them everything that I command you. Do not be dismayed by them, lest I dismay you before them. ¹⁸And I, behold, I make you this day a fortified city, an iron pillar, and bronze walls, against the whole land, against the kings of Judah, its officials, its priests, and the people of the land. ¹⁹They will fight against you, but they shall not prevail against you, for I am with you, declares the LORD, to deliver you."

PORE AND PARAPHRASE

PULL OUT

POSE

PLAN AND PIN

EXODUS 3:10-12

¹⁰*"Therefore, come now, and I will send you to Pharaoh, so that you may bring My people, the sons of Israel, out of Egypt."*

¹¹But Moses said to God, "Who am I, that I should go to Pharaoh, and that I should bring the sons of Israel out of Egypt?"

¹²And He said, "Certainly I will be with you, and this shall be the sign to you that it is I who have sent you: when you have brought the people out of Egypt, you shall worship God at this mountain."

PORE AND PARAPHRASE

PULL OUT

POSE

PLAN AND PIN

Is God calling me to do something I feel unable to handle? How is He confirming His presence with me in this situation?

Not that we are fit (qualified and sufficient in ability) of ourselves to form personal judgments or to claim or count anything as coming from us, but our power and ability and sufficiency are from God. [It is He] Who has qualified us [making us to be fit and worthy and sufficient]. 2 Corinthians 3:5-6, AMP

When I'm surrounded by challenges ...

2 CHRONICLES 20:2-4

²*Then some came and reported to Jehoshaphat, saying, "A great multitude is coming against you from beyond the sea, out of Aram and behold, they are in Hazazon-tamar (that is Engedi)."*

³*Jehoshaphat was afraid and turned his attention to seek the LORD, and proclaimed a fast throughout all Judah.*

⁴*So Judah gathered together to seek help from the LORD; they even came from all the cities of Judah to seek the LORD.*

PORE AND PARAPHRASE

PULL OUT

POSE

PLAN AND PIN

Consider Jehoshaphat's first actions after receiving the news of impending danger. How do they compare with my first reaction to intimidating circumstances?

GROUP DISCUSSION
- *When have you had a "Moses moment," where you weren't sure you could do what God asked you to do?*
- *Why doesn't God always rescue us from the fire?*

DANIEL 3:21-27, HCSB

²¹So these men, in their trousers, robes, head coverings, and other clothes, were tied up and thrown into the furnace of blazing fire. ²²Since the king's command was so urgent and the furnace extremely hot, the raging flames killed those men who carried Shadrach, Meshach, and Abednego up. ²³And these three men, Shadrach, Meshach, and Abednego fell, bound, into the furnace of blazing fire.

²⁴Then King Nebuchadnezzar jumped up in alarm. He said to his advisers, "Didn't we throw three men, bound, into the fire?" "Yes, of course, Your Majesty," they replied to the king.

²⁵He exclaimed, "Look! I see four men, not tied, walking around in the fire unharmed; and the fourth looks like a son of the gods."

²⁶Nebuchadnezzar then approached the door of the furnace of blazing fire and called: "Shadrach, Meshach, and Abednego, you servants of the Most High God—come out!" So Shadrach, Meshach, and Abednego came out of the fire. ... ²⁷They saw that the fire had no effect on the bodies of these men: not a hair of their heads was singed, their robes were unaffected, and there was no smell of fire on them.

PORE AND PARAPHRASE

PULL OUT

POSE

PLAN AND PIN

Am I in the fire right now? If God has chosen not to rescue me from it right now, how have I seen His presence joining me in it?

More Conversation Starters

2 Chronicles 20:6-12; Esther 4:11-16; Psalm 56:11; Jeremiah 1:17-19; 15:20-21; Micah 7:8; Luke 21:15; Acts 6:10; 2 Corinthians 12:9.

TRUSTING GOD WHEN BAD THINGS HAPPEN

"Wherever God in his providence guides you, let it be your joy to know that he is too wise to err—too good to be unkind." —Charles H. Spurgeon [3]

A song of praise to the Lord despite impending devastation in Judah

HABAKKUK 3:17-19, HCSB

[17]*Though there are no sheep in the pen*
  and no cattle in the stalls,
[18]*yet I will triumph in the LORD;*
  I will rejoice in the God of my salvation!
[19]*Yahweh my Lord is my strength;*
  He makes my feet like those of a deer
  and enables me to walk on mountain heights!

PORE AND PARAPHRASE

PULL OUT

POSE

PLAN AND PIN

Consider the prophet's inner peace and confidence in God despite external disaster. What type of famine or ruin have I faced in the past? What about right now? Is my internal confidence with God steady or wavering?

Responding to adversity

GENESIS 37:23-28

²³So it came about, when Joseph reached his brothers, that they stripped Joseph of his tunic, the varicolored tunic that was on him; ²⁴and they took him and threw him into the pit. Now the pit was empty, without any water in it.

²⁵Then they sat down to eat a meal. And as they raised their eyes and looked, behold, a caravan of Ishmaelites was coming from Gilead, with their camels bearing aromatic gum and balm and myrrh, on their way to bring them down to Egypt. ²⁶Judah said to his brothers, "What profit is it for us to kill our brother and cover up his blood? ²⁷Come and let us sell him to the Ishmaelites and not lay our hands on him, for he is our brother, our own flesh." And his brothers listened to him. ²⁸Then some Midianite traders passed by, so they pulled him up and lifted Joseph out of the pit, and sold him to the Ishmaelites for twenty shekels of silver. Thus they brought Joseph into Egypt.

PORE AND PARAPHRASE

PULL OUT

POSE

PLAN AND PIN

Have I been hurt by people I thought loved me? How did their actions result in my imprisonment (emotionally, financially, spiritually, etc.)?

Joseph to his brothers after becoming the chief advisor to the Egyptian Pharaoh

GENESIS 50:20

As for you, you meant evil against me, but God meant it for good in order to bring about this present result, to preserve many people alive.

PORE AND PARAPHRASE

PULL OUT

POSE

PLAN AND PIN

What evil from others has the Lord turned into good in my life?

Job's response to the loss of his children and his wealth

JOB 1:20-22, HCSB

20 Then Job stood up, tore his robe and shaved his head.
 He fell to the ground and worshiped, 21 saying:
  Naked I came from my mother's womb,
  and naked I will leave this life.
  The LORD gives, and the LORD takes away.
  Praise the name of the LORD.
22 Throughout all this Job did not sin or blame God for anything.

PORE AND PARAPHRASE

PULL OUT

POSE

PLAN AND PIN

1 PETER 1:3-6, AMP

³Praised (honored, blessed) be the God and Father of our Lord Jesus Christ (the Messiah)! By His boundless mercy we have been born again to an ever-living hope through the resurrection of Jesus Christ from the dead,

⁴[Born anew] into an inheritance which is beyond the reach of change and decay [imperishable], unsullied and unfading, reserved in heaven for you,

⁵Who are being guarded (garrisoned) by God's power through [your] faith [till you fully inherit that final] salvation that is ready to be revealed [for you] in the last time.

⁶[You should] be exceedingly glad on this account, though now for a little while you may be distressed by trials and suffer temptations.

PORE AND PARAPHRASE

PULL OUT

POSE

PLAN AND PIN

PSALM 28:6-9

⁶*Blessed be the LORD,*
Because He has heard the voice of my supplication.
⁷*The LORD is my strength and my shield;*
My heart trusts in Him, and I am helped;
Therefore my heart exults,
And with my song I shall thank Him.
⁸*The LORD is their strength,*
And He is a saving defense to His anointed.
⁹*Save Your people and bless Your inheritance;*
Be their shepherd also, and carry them forever.

PORE AND PARAPHRASE

PULL OUT

POSE

PLAN AND PIN

More Conversation Starters

Exodus 23:20-23; 2 Samuel 22:32-34; Psalm 5:12; 20:6-8; 27:1-3,13-14; 34:7; Isaiah 59:1-2; 60:1,20; Acts 5:40-42; Romans 5:9; 1 Thessalonians 3:3; Jude 24-25.

Summarize your conversation with God this week. What are the main things the Lord has taught you not only about His love for you but also concerning His desire and ability to protect you? What has been the most meaningful day of conversation have you had this week? Why? What passage has stirred the deepest conversation? At the beginning of this week you wrote down some things that have happened in your life that resulted in you having a shaken confidence in the Lord. How has your conversation with God this week affected your view of why God may have allowed these things and how He was protecting you even while you were going through them?

WEEK FIVE
MY PINK PRINCESS SLIPPERS

FATHER, Open the eyes of my heart. I want to see clearly and come to a full knowledge of who You have declared me to be. I am grateful to know that I know that in You, my past does not define me; my weakness and past performance do not limit me; and the opinions of others do not restrict Your power in my life. I confess my tendency to allow these things to blind me to my identity in You. Thank You for redefining who I am. Please enable me to believe what You have spoken over me. Lord, I want to be enlightened to know the great hope of Your calling me, the glorious riches You have for me, the amazing inheritance that You have given me, and the power that is available to me every day. I refuse to live another day clothed in the very things You died to free me from. This week, as You speak to me through Your Word and whisper to me by Your Spirit, remind me of who I am in You so I can begin to live fully from that place of significance. Uncover the deep hidden recesses of my heart that are filled with the negative and errant strongholds that keep me from recognizing my true identity. Help me to trust in and rely on my God-given image from this day forward. Thank You for taking me from being a pauper to a princess. Now help me to live every day as the royalty that I am in You.

In the name of my Father, the King, **AMEN**

I pray that the eyes of your heart may be enlightened so you may know what is the hope of His calling, what are the glorious riches of His inheritance among the saints, and what is the immeasurable greatness of His power to us who believe, according to the working of His vast strength.
Ephesians 1:18-19, HCSB

MY PINK PRINCESS SLIPPERS

Put on your new nature, and be renewed.
Colossians 3:10, NLT

It's all in the shoes. At least that's what my young friend Ellie thinks.

Her mother, one of my closest friends, named her Elyana. I call her Ellie. She is a six-year-old beauty so full of spunk and vitality that you get tired just watching her. Her name, which conjures up thoughts of elegance and femininity, is an exact description of her personality. Unlike her mom, who much prefers blue jeans and t-shirts, Ellie is a "girly-girl." If it's not uniquely female, Ellie will have nothing to do with it. She is rarely seen in public without her pink glitter-laden slippers, ballerina tutu, or princess crown. These items are staples in her wardrobe and adorning herself with them brings a smile to her face and makes her feel as if there is nothing she can't do. Undeterred by the reaction of those around her at the grocery store, zoo, or neighborhood park, this uninhibited young one desires to dress the way she feels: princess-like. And so every day, with pride and joy, she parades around in her garments of royalty.

Participating in outdoor activities doesn't quell Ellie's passion for female fashion. A recent suggestion that tennis shoes might be better fitted for the day's open-air plans were met by Ellie's staunch rejection. She wouldn't hear of it, not even for a moment. She looked down at her sparkly pink slippers and said, "Mom, these make me run faster!"

Maybe I need Elyana's slippers. It seems that my pace has gotten a little slow. The demands of life seem to be weighing me down and I am not as swift as I used to be. Deadlines, errands, laundry, traffic, ministry obligations, and the upkeep of relationships all seem to be loads ill fitted for these shoulders. Yet I often continue to hoist more on them then they can handle. The result: a slow, breathless, uncomfortable swagger that keeps me from living life to the full and running at a Spirit-filled pace.

Ellie seems to have the answer for my problem. If it only took a pair of the right shoes for her to get a new kick in her step then maybe that's exactly what I need: a quick change in attire. What about Ellie's glittery slippers, unsteady at their soles and wobbly in their cushioned coverings, could possibly assist her in achieving her desired speed? Couldn't have been the shoes in and of themselves. Maybe it was just what they represented that made her legs move a little more swiftly. Those dolled-up house slippers boosted her esteem as they declared her status of royalty in every activity of her life. Each time one foot crossed in front of the other she saw another glimpse of her stunning princess attire and her princess attitude was evoked and reinforced. The result: her steps got lighter and her speed swifter.

I've been schooled by a six-year-old. I'm reminded that to move with agility in the whirlwind and often mundane activities of this life I need to change my shoes; that life *in this world* will be better if it is lived with a power *beyond this world*. I've been wearing attire that is not suited for the likes of a woman whose Father is the Most High King. I often wear them when it's "acceptable" but seem to take them off when the activities seem to call for something more suitable. Repressed by other's opinions, I've been wearing clothes that are more socially acceptable but detrimental to my spiritual growth. So, starting today, I'm changing my entire wardrobe, taking off the old grubs and exchanging them for the new.

Self-pity has been thrown in the recycle bin. In its place, I'm wearing the song that my Father sings over me. *(See Zepheniah 3:14-17.)*

The backbreaking garment of guilt is no longer slung over my shoulders. Instead, I'm clothed with His promise of newness. *(See Isaiah 43:18-19.)*

He's replaced the ill-fitting covering of wickedness with an eternal robe of righteousness. *(See Isaiah 61:10.)*

The wandering imaginations of my mind have been restored with the mind of Christ. *(See 1 Corinthians 2:16.)*

That unstoppable pride, the heaviest load of all, has been thrown away. In its place I'm putting on the humility of Christ Himself. *(See Philippians 2:3-7.)*

There's a lifting of my head, a feather-like weight to my step, and a new recognition of my position in Him that I'm walking in now. It's a feeling that I'm growing accustomed to and never like to live without. I like these clothes. They fit me nicely. I think I'll wear them even when someone says I should put on something else.

You can have them if you like. They are yours for the asking. (See James 1:5.)

THIS WEEK, HAVE A CONVERSATION WITH GOD.

Do I allow God's Word or some other standard to define me? What negative tendencies, mentalities, and strongholds do I need to "take off"? During what type of circumstances do I tend to forget who I am in Christ? What truths from Scripture do I need to "put on" and keep on every day? How will I respond differently in my life's situations when I believe what the Scripture says about me?

> "'Set your hearts on things above' (v. 1) is *ta anō zēteite*, and
> 'Set your minds on things above' (v. 2) is *ta anō phroneite*.
> The first suggests striving; the second suggests concentrating." [1]

COLOSSIANS 3:1-10, NIV

[1]Since, then, you have been raised with Christ, set your hearts on things above, where Christ is seated at the right hand of God. [2]Set your minds on things above, not on earthly things. [3]For you died, and your life is now hidden with Christ in God. [4]When Christ, who is your life, appears, then you also will appear with him in glory.

[5]Put to death, therefore, whatever belongs to your earthly nature: sexual immorality, impurity, lust, evil desires and greed, which is idolatry. [6]Because of these, the wrath of God is coming. [7]You used to walk in these ways, in the life you once lived. [8]But now you must rid yourselves of all such things as these: anger, rage, malice, slander, and filthy language from your lips. [9]Do not lie to each other, since you have taken off your old self with its practices [10]and have put on the new self, which is being renewed in knowledge in the image of its Creator.

PORE AND PARAPHRASE

PULL OUT

POSE

PLAN AND PIN

SET (*zēteite*) means "to seek or strive for earnestly" [2]

GROUP DISCUSSION

- *How do you "put to death" the worldly things Paul described in Colossians 3?*
- *What are you "wearing" that keeps you bogged down instead of looking up to the Lord?*

THE TRUTH ABOUT ME

If anyone is in Christ, he is a new creation.
The old has passed away; behold, the new has come.
2 Corinthians 5:17, ESV

I am a masterpiece

Paul describing the divine calling by God to the Christians at Ephesus

EPHESIANS 2:10
We are His workmanship, created in Christ Jesus for good works,
which God prepared beforehand so that we would walk in them.

> The word WORKMANSHIP *(poiema)* is used only here and in
> Romans 1:20, where the NIV renders it "what has been made."
> *Poiema* denotes a work of art or divine masterpiece. [3]

PORE AND PARAPHRASE

PULL OUT

POSE

PLAN AND PIN

Consider the word *workmanship*, its meaning, and how it is used in Romans 1:20.
What are some things that this word brings to mind?

I am hand chosen by God ...

... to be blessed

EPHESIANS 1:3-4, NLT

³All praise to God, the Father of our Lord Jesus Christ, who has blessed us with every spiritual blessing in the heavenly realms because we are united with Christ. ⁴Even before he made the world, God loved us and chose us in Christ to be holy and without fault in his eyes.

PORE AND PARAPHRASE

PULL OUT

POSE

PLAN AND PIN

How do the feelings of being rejected compare to the feelings of knowing God chose me?

GROUP DISCUSSION
- *Do you feel justified, chosen, and forgiven? How would you live differently if you believed you were all of these things?*

... to know Him and proclaim His excellencies

2 PETER 1:3

... seeing that His divine power has granted to us everything pertaining to life and godliness, through the true knowledge of Him who called us by His own glory and excellence.

1 PETER 2:9

But you are A CHOSEN RACE, A royal PRIESTHOOD, A HOLY NATION, A PEOPLE FOR God's OWN POSSESSION, so that you may proclaim the excellencies of Him who has called you out of darkness into His marvelous light.

PORE AND PARAPHRASE

PULL OUT

POSE

PLAN AND PIN

God chose believers for the purpose of revealing His love to mankind. What does this verse reveal is the purpose for my calling into royalty and holiness? What specifically might I do today to serve this purpose?

... to be a friend of God

JOHN 15:15-16, NLT

15I no longer call you slaves, because a master doesn't confide in his slaves. Now you are my friends, since I have told you everything the Father told me. 16You didn't choose me. I chose you. I appointed you to go and produce lasting fruit, so that the Father will give you whatever you ask for, using my name.

PORE AND PARAPHRASE

PULL OUT

POSE

PLAN AND PIN

> Notice that Jesus linked request-making to fruit-bearing. The answering of prayers is specifically tied to the production of eternal fruit. [4]

What do these verses reveal are some of the benefits of being a chosen, appointed, friend of God?

I am fully forgiven

COLOSSIANS 1:21-22, NLT

²¹*This includes you who were once far away from God. You were his enemies, separated from him by your evil thoughts and actions, ²²yet now he has brought you back as his friends. He has done this through his death on the cross in his own human body. As a result, he has brought you into the very presence of God, and you are holy and blameless as you stand before him without a single fault.*

PORE AND PARAPHRASE

PULL OUT

POSE

PLAN AND PIN

Verse 22 declares: (1) I am **welcome** in God's presence (reconciled). (2) I am **holy.** (3) I am **blameless**—standing before Him without one single fault. Which one of these is the easiest/hardest for me to accept? Why?

More Conversation Starters

Genesis 1:26-27,31; 2:22; Exodus 19:5-6; 1 Samuel 16:7; Isaiah 61:1-6; Jeremiah 29:11-13; John 1:12; 15:16,19; Romans 5:10-11; 8:1-2; 2 Corinthians 5:18-21; Ephesians 1:4; 2:4-9,19; Philippians 3:8-11; Hebrews 13:20-21.

THE TRUTH ABOUT ME, CONTINUED

I am necessary

Paul writing to encourage believers of their individual significance within the body of Christ

ROMANS 12:4-6

⁴For just as we have many members in one body and all the members do not have the same function, ⁵so we, who are many, are one body in Christ, and individually members one of another. ⁶Since we have gifts that differ according to the grace given to us, each of us is to exercise them accordingly.

PORE AND PARAPHRASE

PULL OUT

POSE

PLAN AND PIN

What is my God-given gift? How am I using that gift right now within the body of Christ? Is my goal in using it to edify others or to garner attention and praise for myself?

Do I have a tendency to desire a different gift than the one I have been given? Why? How do others make me feel insignificant?

I am valuable

LUKE 12:6-7, ESV

⁶Are not five sparrows sold for two pennies? And not one of them is forgotten before God. ⁷Why, even the hairs of your head are all numbered. Fear not; you are of more value than many sparrows.

In the markets of Jerusalem, a SPARROW was sold cheaply—two for a penny. If two penny's worth was purchased, the fifth was thrown in for free. In essence, the fifth sparrow had no value. [5]

PORE AND PARAPHRASE

PULL OUT

POSE

PLAN AND PIN

Consider the "fifth sparrow" in light of the last part of verse 6. When have I ever felt as if I had no value? How does this passage speak to me regarding that situation?

EPHESIANS 2:19, AMP

Therefore you are no longer outsiders (exiles, migrants, and aliens, excluded from the rights of citizens), but you now share citizenship with the saints (God's own people, consecrated and set apart for Himself) and you belong to God's [own] household.

PORE AND PARAPHRASE

PULL OUT

POSE

PLAN AND PIN

I am delightful

ZEPHANIAH 3:17, HCSB

The LORD your God is among you, a warrior who saves. He will rejoice over you with gladness. He will bring you quietness with His love. He will delight in you with shouts of joy.

PORE AND PARAPHRASE

PULL OUT

POSE

PLAN AND PIN

More Conversation Starters

Genesis 1:26-27,31; Deuteronomy 30:9; Job 31:15; Isaiah 62:5; 1 Corinthians 6:19-20; 12:4-27; Ephesians 2:12; 3:6; 4:16; Philippians 1:6; 3:20; 1 Peter 4:10.

DAY FOUR

CHANGING CLOTHES— TAKING OFF THE OLD

We do not have the excuse of ignorance, everything—and I do mean every-thing—connected with that old way of life has to go. It's rotten through and through. Get rid of it! And then take on an entirely new way of life—a God-fash-ioned life, a life renewed from the inside and working itself into your conduct as God accurately reproduces his character in you. Ephesians 4:22-24, MSG

ISAIAH 43:18-19

¹⁸*"Do not call to mind the former things,*
Or ponder things of the past.
¹⁹*Behold, I will do something new.*
Now it will spring forth;
Will you not be aware of it?
I will even make a roadway in the wilderness,
Rivers in the desert."

PORE AND PARAPHRASE

PULL OUT

POSE

PLAN AND PIN

What new thing would I welcome in my life right now? What former things do I need to banish from my thoughts?

EPHESIANS 4:22-24, NLT

²²Throw off your old sinful nature and your former way of life, which is corrupted by lust and deception. ²³Instead, let the Spirit renew your thoughts and attitudes. ²⁴Put on your new nature, created to be like God—truly righteous and holy.

PORE AND PARAPHRASE

PULL OUT

POSE

PLAN AND PIN

> See to it that no one takes you captive through philosophy and empty deception, according to the tradition of men, according to the elementary principles of the world, rather than according to Christ. Colossians 2:8

GROUP DISCUSSION--
- *What process must we go through to "throw off" the old way of life?*
- *How would you advise a new Christian to "put on" the new nature?*

ROMANS 6:12-14, ESV

12Let not sin therefore reign in your mortal bodies, to make you obey their passions. 13Do not present your members to sin as instruments for unrighteousness, but present yourselves to God as those who have been brought from death to life, and your members to God as instruments for righteousness. 14For sin will have no dominion over you, since you are not under law but under grace.

PORE AND PARAPHRASE

PULL OUT

POSE

PLAN AND PIN

Consider this passage in The Message translation below. Throughout the course of your day, in what way do you "run little errands" that are connected with your old way of life?

> That means you must not give sin a vote in the way you conduct your lives. Don't give it the time of day. Don't even run little errands that are connected with that old way of life. Throw yourselves wholeheartedly and full-time— remember, you've been raised from the dead!—into God's way of doing things. Sin can't tell you how to live. After all, you're not living under that old tyranny any longer. You're living in the freedom of God. Romans 6:12-14, MSG

GALATIANS 5:16-21

[16]But I say, walk by the Spirit, and you will not carry out the desire of the flesh. [17]For the flesh sets its desire against the Spirit, and the Spirit against the flesh; for these are in opposition to one another, so that you may not do the things that you please. [18]But if you are led by the Spirit, you are not under the Law. [19]Now the deeds of the flesh are evident, which are: immorality, impurity, sensuality, [20]idolatry, sorcery, enmities, strife, jealousy, outbursts of anger, disputes, dissensions, factions, [21]envying, drunkenness, carousing, and things like these, of which I forewarn you, just as I have forewarned you, that those who practice such things will not inherit the kingdom of God.

PORE AND PARAPHRASE

PULL OUT

POSE

PLAN AND PIN

Consider the deeds of the flesh listed in the passage. Rate yourself in each area with 15 being the one you struggle with the least and 1 being the one you most contend with. Today, have a conversation with God about the top two on your list. What would He have you to do to begin to deal with those?

More Conversation Starters

Romans 6:5-8,16; 7:4-6; 8:6,11; Galatians 2:20; Ephesians 2:3; 5:9-10,18; Philippians 3:12-14; Colossians 2:11; 3:8-10; Titus 3:3-5; Hebrews 12:1; James 1:14-15.

CHANGING CLOTHES— PUTTING ON THE NEW

Buy your clothes from me, clothes designed in Heaven.
You've gone around half-naked long enough.
Revelation 3:18, MSG

GALATIANS 5:22-25

²²*The fruit of the Spirit is love, joy, peace, patience, kindness, goodness, faithfulness,* ²³*gentleness, self-control; against such things there is no law.*
²⁴*Now those who belong to Christ Jesus have crucified the flesh with its passions and desires.*
    ²⁵*If we live by the Spirit, let us also walk by the Spirit.*

PORE AND PARAPHRASE

PULL OUT

POSE

PLAN AND PIN

Consider the fruit of the Spirit. Rate each area with 9 being the one that is least evidenced in my life and 1 being the one most clearly seen. What would God have me do today to begin to practice those fruit of the Spirit?

COLOSSIANS 3:1-10, ESV

¹If then you have been raised with Christ, seek the things that are above, where Christ is, seated at the right hand of God. ²Set your minds on things that are above, not on things that are on earth. ³For you have died, and your life is hidden with Christ in God. ⁴When Christ who is your life appears, then you also will appear with him in glory. ⁵Put to death therefore what is earthly in you: sexual immorality, impurity, passion, evil desire, and covetousness, which is idolatry. ⁶On account of these the wrath of God is coming. ⁷In these you too once walked, when you were living in them. ⁸But now you must put them all away: anger, wrath, malice, slander, and obscene talk from your mouth. ⁹Do not lie to one another, seeing that you have put off the old self with its practices ¹⁰and have put on the new self, which is being renewed in knowledge after the image of its creator.

PORE AND PARAPHRASE

PULL OUT

POSE

PLAN AND PIN

Examine some practical ways today that I can put on the new self following Paul's instructions to: 1) Seek the things above. 2) Set my mind on things eternal. 3) Put to death what is earthly. 4) Put away deeds of the flesh.

2 TIMOTHY 1:7,9

⁷For God has not given us a spirit of timidity, but of power and love and discipline.
⁹[God] has saved us and called us with a holy calling, not according to our works, but according to His own purpose and grace which was granted us in Christ Jesus from all eternity

PORE AND PARAPHRASE

PULL OUT

POSE

PLAN AND PIN

In what areas of your life am I walking in fear right now? How do the God-given gifts listed at the end of verse 7 and in verse 9 help to replace that fear?

MATTHEW 5:13-16

¹³"You are the salt of the earth; but if the salt has become tasteless, how can it be made salty again? It is no longer good for anything, except to be thrown out and trampled under foot by men.
¹⁴You are the light of the world. A city set on a hill cannot be hidden; ¹⁵nor does anyone light a lamp and put it under a basket, but on the lampstand, and it gives light to all who are in the house. ¹⁶Let your light shine before men in such a way that they may see your good works, and glorify your Father who is in heaven."

PORE AND PARAPHRASE

PULL OUT

POSE

PLAN AND PIN

How can I be be salt and light today? What will be most difficult about this? Who will be my biggest detractor?

More Conversation Starters
Ezekiel 36:26; Luke 9:23-24; Romans 6:8-14,19; 8:29; 12:1-2; 13:12-14; 2 Corinthians 3:17-18; Ephesians 2:1-10; 4:22-23; Philippians 3:12-13; Colossians 3:10; 1 John 3:2.

Summarize your conversation with God this week. In what specific ways have you been challenged to renew your mind in regard to your identity in Christ? What have you been challenged to "take off" and "put on"? What practical steps do you plan to take to make this happen? What has been the most meaningful day of conversation have you had this week? Why? What verse has stirred the deepest conversation?

GROUP DISCUSSION
- *Which fruit of the Spirit is the most prevalent in your life? On which do you need to work the most?*
- *What is encompassed by a spirit of power and discipline?*

BONUS SECTION

These passages have been a great help to me as I seek daily to "put on" spiritual clothes that will cause me to walk worthy of my calling in Christ. Detach them, copy them, even share them; but whatever you do, USE them to help you take off the old and put on the new!

IDENTITY IN CHRIST

- I am a child of God (John 1:12).
- I have peace with God (Rom. 5:1).
- The Holy Spirit lives in me (1 Cor. 3:16).
- I have access to God's wisdom (Jas. 1:5).
- I am helped by God (Heb. 4:16).
- I am reconciled to God (Rom. 5:11).
- I am not condemned by God (Rom. 8:1).
- I am justified (Rom. 5:1).
- I have Christ's righteousness (Rom. 5:19; 2 Cor. 5:21).
- I am Christ's ambassador (2 Cor. 5:20).
- I am completely forgiven (Col. 1:13-14).
- I am tenderly loved by God (Jer. 31:3).
- I am the sweet fragrance of Christ to God (2 Cor. 2:15).
- I am a temple in which God dwells (1 Cor. 3:16).
- I am blameless and beyond reproach (Col. 1:22).
- I am the salt of the earth (Matt. 5:13).
- I am the light of the world (Matt. 5:14).
- I am a branch on Christ's vine (John 15:1,5).
- I am God's friend (Prov. 3:32).
- I am chosen by Christ to bear fruit (John 15:6).
- I am a joint heir with Christ, sharing His inheritance with Him (Rom. 8:17).
- I am united to the Lord, one spirit with Him (1 Cor. 6:17).
- I am a member of Christ's body (1 Cor. 12:27).
- I am a saint (Rom. 1:7).

- I am hidden with Christ in God (Col. 3:3).
- I am chosen by God, holy, and dearly loved (Col. 3:12).
- I am a child of the light (1 Thess. 5:5).
- I am holy, and I share in God's heavenly calling (Heb. 3:1).
- I am sanctified (Heb. 2:11).
- I am one of God's living stones, being built up in Christ as a spiritual house (1 Pet. 2:5).
- I am a member of a chosen race, a royal priesthood, a holy nation, a people for God's own possession and created to sing His praises (1 Pet. 2:9-10).
- I am firmly rooted and built up in Christ (Col. 2:7).
- I am born of God, and the Evil One cannot touch me (1 John 5:18).
- I have the mind of Christ (1 Cor. 2:16).
- I may approach God with boldness, freedom, and confidence (Eph. 3:12).
- I have been rescued from Satan's domain and transferred into the kingdom of Christ (Col. 1:13).
- I have been made complete in Christ (Col. 2:10).
- I have been given a spirit of power, love, and self-discipline (2 Tim. 1:7).
- I have been given great and precious promises by God (2 Pet. 1:4).
- God meets my needs (Phil. 4:19).
- I am a princess in God's kingdom (John 1:12; 1 Tim. 6:15).
- I have been bought with a price, and I belong to God (1 Cor. 6:19-20).
- I have been adopted as God's child (Eph. 1:5).
- I have direct access to God through the Holy Spirit (Eph. 2:18).
- I am assured that all things are working together for good (Rom. 8:28).
- I am free from any condemning charges against me (Rom. 8:31).
- I cannot be separated from the love of God (Rom. 8:35).
- I have been established, anointed, and sealed by God (2 Cor. 1:21-22).
- I am confident that the good work that God has begun in me will be perfected (Phil. 1:6).
- I am a citizen of heaven (Phil. 3:20).
- I am a personal witness of Christ's (Acts 1:8).
- I am God's coworker (1 Cor. 3:9; 2 Cor. 6:1).
- I am seated with Christ in the heavenly realm (Eph. 2:6).
- I am God's workmanship (Eph. 2:10).
- I can do all things through Christ, who gives me the strength I need (Phil. 4:13).

THE **HOLE** UNDER THE DOOR

LORD, I desire to be a useful and relevant tool for Your purposes in this generation. Give me eyes to see the ways that I have been influenced by this culture, causing me to become apathetic and passive regarding Your plans for me. Forgive me for allowing the things of this world to replace my fervent desire for the things that are eternal. I want a restored passionate relationship with You, one in which I can be used for Your glory. I do not want to be on the shelf, unable to be an efficient servant of Yours because I am lukewarm. Forgive me of the sin of indifference and complacency. Give me a renewed sensitivity to the things that matter to You. Will You reignite the fire and passion between us this week? As I press into You, open my spiritual eyes to see the holes I have left unguarded to the world and its influences. Reveal to me the spirits of this age that creep in, affecting my friendship with You, and show me the places they enter. As we talk this week, give me Your courage to do whatever is necessary to fix the holes by severing relationships with anyone and anything assisting in keeping us from experiencing sweet intimacy and fellowship. Thank You for knocking on the door of my heart. I am listening for Your arrival and will answer Your call quickly and in full obedience.

In Jesus' name, **AMEN.**

"I know you inside and out, and find little to my liking. You're not cold, you're not hot—far better to be either cold or hot! You're stale. You're stagnant. You make me want to vomit. You brag, 'I'm rich, I've got it made, I need nothing from anyone,' oblivious that in fact you're a pitiful, blind beggar, threadbare and homeless. Here's what I want you to do: Buy your gold from me, gold that's been through the refiner's fire. Then you'll be rich. Buy your clothes from me, clothes designed in Heaven. You've gone around half-naked long enough. And buy medicine for your eyes from me so you can see, really see."
Revelation 3:15-18, MSG

THE HOLE UNDER THE DOOR

I know your deeds, that you are neither cold nor hot; I wish that you were cold or hot. So because you are lukewarm, and neither hot nor cold, I will spit you out of My mouth. Revelation 3:15-16

I noticed it almost immediately—the hole under the door.

I often have my quiet time in my bedroom, sometimes sitting on the bed or kneeling by my open window. Today, after asking the Lord to speak clearly during our time together, I felt prompted to lie flat. Turning my head to the side brought my vision directly in line with the base of the door in my bedroom that leads to the outdoor patio (where my children's sandboxes and Tyke toys are scattered everywhere, keeping me from having the manicured landscaping I've always wanted). In the center, between the door's bottom edge and the carpeted bedroom floor, was a hole. The insulation designed to keep out the cold air of winter and the heat of the summer had begun to disintegrate. Years of swinging the door open and closed to access the backyard had rubbed the insulation harshly, causing it to no longer supply adequate padding. Attempting to ignore this seemingly trivial and unspiritual interruption to my quiet time, I closed my eyes and tried to refocus. But I couldn't ...

"There's a hole under the door."

The Holy Spirit's voice resonated deep within me. I remembered the hot Texas summer months when my bedroom hadn't offered a cool place of solace because it was the hottest room in the house. Even with our air conditioner turned on high, this room was still uncomfortably warm. And this January morning brought some of the coldest days that Dallas would probably see for the year, and my bedroom was never quite warm enough as the cold air seeped into the room. I huddled cozily into the warm terrycloth robe my mother had purchased me for Christmas as a wisp of wintry air from outside crept in and swept across my face. All those months of trying to figure out why our bedroom wasn't ever fully warm or fully cool made sense now. I had found the culprit—the hole under the door.

The great theologian and philosopher Francis Schaeffer said, "The evangelical church has become seduced by the world spirit of this present age." [1] An older woman in the faith reminded me of this recently. This mentor looked me squarely in the eyes to give me a stern and frank talk about the crafty influences of this world. In her wisdom, she challenged me to always remember that I was a part of the church, and I must beware of the crafty seduction by way of unnoticed impressions that the world and its influences have on even well-guarded Christians. This cunning influence inconspicuously and delicately seeps, unseen and unnoticed, through the holes we have left unguarded. The result: a spiritual thermostat that reads "lukewarm" and creates an atmosphere that is not leaning to either extreme necessary for spiritual usefulness.

Was this what the Holy Spirit was saying to the church of Laodicea as recorded in Revelation 3? This church, the last of the seven to be addressed, was admonished to hear and obey the Spirit's message. Refusal to do this would result in a removal of the very presence and power of God from their midst. When the time came to address the specific needs of this church body, the Spirit spoke of their inability to be used by God because of their "lukewarm" temperature. In no uncertain terms, He made clear that they would have to be set aside until they determined to choose an extreme: the fire of holy passion and the coolness of Christlikeness. Either extreme—red hot or icy cold—could be used by God, but being lukewarm wasn't an acceptable option. The middle ground of mediocrity—halfhearted indifference, passivity, and inaction—weakened their effectiveness and diluted their usefulness.

The reality of this passage came to life in my mind's eye. In our modest Dallas home, the master bedroom had become the least used room in the whole house because, like Laodicea, it had holes that needed to be fixed. When I needed a warm haven from winter air or a refreshing cool retreat on a heated summer Texas day, my room had nothing to offer. What had caused this church to become useless? Apparently, the same thing that had stunted the potential of my bedroom: the crafty spirits of the age seeping in through the hole under their spiritual door. The writer puts it this way in Revelation 3:17—"For you say, I am rich, I have prospered, and I need nothing, not realizing that you are wretched, pitiable, poor, blind, and naked" (ESV).

Thirty-five years prior to this letter, an earthquake had destroyed Laodicea and the city's resources had established their recovery. As a result, they had begun to trust in what they could do for themselves rather than what Christ had done for them and wanted to do through them. Like an alarm clock breaking the silence of the spiritual night and jarring these believers awake from their slumber, the spirit of the age seeping into this church was revealed. Instead of trusting in the divine riches they had discovered in

Christ, they placed faith in the physical wealth they had acquired. They became blind to their own depravity and need for more than what their money could buy. The cool breeze of self-sufficiency was seeping into the church and chilling the temperature of their relationship with God.

I couldn't move from my prostrate position as the same Spirit who spoke to the believers at Laodicea 2,000 years ago now spoke clearly to me: "You belong to My church, Priscilla, and you are the very temple of the living God. Watch for the holes the subtle spirits of this age use to seep in and corrupt the purity of our relationship."

As I stared at the glaring physical illustration of this deep spiritual principle, I began to feel the Spirit's soothing conviction as the holes in my "church" and the effect they had caused were revealed. I saw clearly the "hole" of that movie and magazine, television program and idle time, book and relationship had been opportune openings. And the world's spirits, cunning and crafty as they are, were causing my judgment to become slightly impaired, my spiritual vision partially blocked, and my ambitions leaning toward fleshly.

As clearly as my physical eyes could see the hole under the door in my bedroom, the Spirit allowed my spiritual eyes to see the fissures that were keeping my relationship with Christ mild tempered, passive, and, at times, plain old worldly.

After my quiet time, I called a contractor to fix the problem with my bedroom door. By the time she came, another major renovation had already begun. The Contractor of my soul had arrived to help me begin to patch up the holes in my life so that I could be used by God—to be warmth to a cold, dying soul, or cool breath of fresh Christlike air to those scorched and in need. I want to be ready for His service; standing at attention, ready for action, and prepared for His call to engage.

THIS WEEK, HAVE A CONVERSATION WITH GOD.

Take a personal spiritual inventory: Am I "lukewarm" (passive, indifferent, complacent) in my relationship with the Lord? Was there a time when I was on fire for Him, when I was being used by Him to accomplish His purposes? What "spirits of the age" have begun to seep into my life unnoticed, causing the temperature change in my spiritual life? What "holes" need to be patched? How can I start the repair these holes?

The Spirit of God to the believers in Laodicea

REVELATION 3:15-20, NLT

[15]*"I know all the things you do, that you are neither hot nor cold. I wish that you were one or the other!* [16]*But since you are like lukewarm water, neither hot nor cold, I will spit you out of my mouth!* [17]*You say, 'I am rich. I have everything I want. I don't need a thing!' And you don't realize that you are wretched and miserable and poor and blind and naked.* [18]*So I advise you to buy gold from me—gold that has been purified by fire. Then you will be rich. Also buy white garments from me so you will not be shamed by your nakedness, and ointment for your eyes so you will be able to see.* [19]*I correct and discipline everyone I love. So be diligent and turn from your indifference.*

[20]*Look! I stand at the door and knock. If you hear my voice and open the door, I will come in, and we will share a meal together as friends."*

PORE AND PARAPHRASE

PULL OUT

POSE

PLAN AND PIN

GROUP DISCUSSION
- *What characterizes a lukewarm Christian?*
- *What "holes under the door" have allowed in messages that water down your faith?*

THE LUKEWARM BELIEVER

You did not go up to the gaps or restore the wall around the house of Israel so that it might stand in battle on the day of the LORD.
Ezekiel 13:5, HCSB

Short-lived love

HAGGAI 1:2-9, ESV

²"Thus says the LORD of hosts: These people say the time has not yet come to rebuild the house of the LORD." ³Then the word of the LORD came by the hand of Haggai the prophet, ⁴"Is it a time for you yourselves to dwell in your paneled houses, while this house lies in ruins? ⁵Now, therefore, thus says the LORD of hosts: Consider your ways. ⁶You have sown much, and harvested little. You eat, but you never have enough; you drink, but you never have your fill. You clothe yourselves, but no one is warm. And he who earns wages does so to put them into a bag with holes. ⁷Thus says the LORD of hosts: Consider your ways. ⁸Go up to the hills and bring wood and build the house, that I may take pleasure in it and that I may be glorified, says the LORD. ⁹You looked for much, and behold, it came to little. And when you brought it home, I blew it away. Why? declares the LORD of hosts. Because of my house that lies in ruins, while each of you busies himself with his own house."

PORE AND PARAPHRASE

Haggai delivered his message to the Israelites in 520 B.C., approximately 16 years after they had returned with the intention of rebuilding the temple of the Lord. ²

PULL OUT

POSE

PLAN AND PIN

Consider the cause of the people's lack of passion for God's priority of rebuilding the temple and the consequences of their indifference. What personal agenda has cooled my zeal to accomplish God's priorities for me? What consequences am I facing?

HOSEA 6:4-6, MSG

4"What am I to do with you, Ephraim?
    What do I make of you, Judah?
Your declarations of love last no longer
    than morning mist and predawn dew.
5That's why I use prophets to shake you to attention,
    why my words cut you to the quick:
To wake you up to my judgment
    blazing like light.
6I'm after love that lasts, not more religion.
    I want you to know God, not go to more prayer meetings.

PORE AND PARAPHRASE

PULL OUT

POSE

PLAN AND PIN

What is the normal pattern of my relationship with the Lord: wavering, loyal, lasting, conditional? Is it my normal tendency to display my loyalty to the Lord through my devotion to know Him and spend time with Him or by participating in religious activity?

The elders of Israel to Samuel the prophet

1 SAMUEL 8:5-9

⁵And they said to him, "Behold, you have grown old, and your sons do not walk in your ways. Now appoint a king for us to judge us like all the nations." ⁶But the thing was displeasing in the sight of Samuel when they said, "Give us a king to judge us." And Samuel prayed to the LORD. ⁷The LORD said to Samuel, "Listen to the voice of the people in regard to all that they say to you, for they have not rejected you, but they have rejected Me from being king over them. ⁸Like all the deeds which they have done since the day that I brought them up from Egypt even to this day—in that they have forsaken Me and served other gods—so they are doing to you also. ⁹Now then, listen to their voice; however, you shall solemnly warn them and tell them of the procedure of the king who will reign over them."

PORE AND PARAPHRASE

PULL OUT

POSE

PLAN AND PIN

Consider 1 Samuel 8:19-20 below. Why did the people want an earthly king? What do you have a tendency to desire simply to be more closely associated with those around you? How have you seen this reflected in the American Christianity?

> "We must have a king over us. Then we'll be like all the other nations: our king will judge us, go out before us, and fight our battles." 1 Samuel 8:19-20, HCSB

More Conversation Starters
Leviticus 26:18-20; Deuteronomy 28:38-40; Judges 5:13-18; Ecclesiastes 9:10; Jeremiah 9:3; Amos 4:6-11; Matthew 13:13-15; John 12:4-6; Revelation 2:4; 3:15.

GROUP DISCUSSION
- *Are there times when you put wanting to be like the world above wanting to be more like Christ? When and how?*
- *What are some practical ways we can pursue the calling of Hosea 6:6? What is the difference between "religion" and "a love that lasts" as described in this verse?*

RECOGNIZING THE HOLES

Don't you realize that friendship with the world makes you an enemy of God? I say it again: If you want to be a friend of the world, you make yourself an enemy of God. James 4:4, NLT

The spirit of the age comes in through false teaching

2 TIMOTHY 3:1-7, ESV

[1]But understand this, that in the last days there will come times of difficulty. [2]For people will be lovers of self, lovers of money, proud, arrogant, abusive, disobedient to their parents, ungrateful, unholy, [3]heartless, unappeasable, slanderous, without self-control, brutal, not loving good, [4]treacherous, reckless, swollen with conceit, lovers of pleasure rather than lovers of God, [5]having the appearance of godliness, but denying its power. Avoid such people. [6]For among them are those who creep into households and capture weak women, burdened with sins and led astray by various passions, [7]always learning and never able to arrive at a knowledge of the truth.

PORE AND PARAPHRASE

PULL OUT

POSE

PLAN AND PIN

Consider the 19 worldly characteristics listed by Paul in this passage. Have any of these begun to seep into my heart and life? Pinpoint the "hole under the door" through which they are entering.

The spirit of the age comes in through the culture

A reminder to God's chosen people to remain set apart from Canaan

LEVITICUS 20:22-24,26

[22]"You are therefore to keep all My statutes and all My ordinances and do them, so that the land to which I am bringing you to live will not spew you out. [23]Moreover, you shall not follow the customs of the nation which I will drive out before you, for they did all these things, and therefore I have abhorred them. [24]Hence I have said to you, 'You are to possess their land, and I Myself will give it to you to possess it, a land flowing with milk and honey.' I am the LORD your God, who has separated you from the peoples. [26]Thus you are to be holy to Me, for I the LORD am holy; and I have set you apart from the peoples to be Mine."

PORE AND PARAPHRASE

PULL OUT

POSE

PLAN AND PIN

"When the Jews arrived in Canaan ... they did not know how to build, to perform arts, or even to farm adequately ... The Canaanites were sophisticated and successful by comparison, and seemed to know what should be done to ensure good crops ... such feelings of inferiority were aided and abetted by excuses for sexual license." [3]

Why would it be difficult to maintain a separation between the Israelites and Canaanites? What are the difficulties I face in maintaining separation between myself/my family and the culture?

1 CORINTHIANS 15:33-34, ESV

33Do not be deceived: "Bad company ruins good morals." 34Wake up from your drunken stupor, as is right, and do not go on sinning. For some have no knowledge of God. I say this to your shame.

PORE AND PARAPHRASE

PULL OUT

POSE

PLAN AND PIN

Do your close relationships foster a full commitment in my relationship with God or contribute to a weakened and half-hearted spiritual dedication?

The spirit of the age comes in through materialism

MARK 4:18-19, AMP

18And the [seeds] sown among the thorns are others who hear the Word;
19Then the cares and anxieties of the world and distractions of the age, and the pleasure and delight and false glamour and deceitfulness of riches, and the craving and passionate desire for other things creep in and choke and suffocate the Word, and it becomes fruitless.

PORE AND PARAPHRASE

PULL OUT

POSE

PLAN AND PIN

MATTHEW 26:14-16

[14]*Then one of the twelve, named Judas Iscariot, went to the chief priests* [15]*and said, "What are you willing to give me to betray Him to you?" And they weighed out thirty pieces of silver to him.* [16]*From then on he began looking for a good opportunity to betray Jesus.*

PORE AND PARAPHRASE

PULL OUT

POSE

PLAN AND PIN

Was there a time in my life when my desire for worldly possessions caused me to use others at any cost to get what I wanted or to compromise my faith to have it? If so, how did that affect my relationship with others and with Christ?

More Conversations Starters

Matthew 13:3-9; 20:17-19; Mark 4:18-19; Romans 1:28-32; 16:17-18; 1 Corinthians 5:6; Ephesians 4:14-15; 1 Thessalonians 5:5-6; Philippians 1:27; 2 Timothy 1:13; Jude 1:3-12.

THE CALL TO ACT

"Stay awake and pray, so that you won't enter into temptation. The spirit is willing, but the flesh is weak." Matthew 26:41, HCSB

Stand at attention and be alert

EPHESIANS 6:10-11,13-18, HCSB

¹⁰*Finally, be strengthened by the Lord and by His vast strength.* ¹¹*Put on the full armor of God so that you can stand against the tactics of the Devil. ...* ¹³*This is why you must take up the full armor of God, so that you may be able to resist in the evil day, and having prepared everything, to take your stand.* ¹⁴*Stand, therefore,*
>*with truth like a belt around your waist,*
>*righteousness like armor on your chest,*
>¹⁵*and your feet sandaled with readiness for the gospel of peace.*
>¹⁶*In every situation take the shield of faith,*
>*and with it you will be able to extinguish*
>*the flaming arrows of the evil one.*
>¹⁷*Take the helmet of salvation,*
>*and the sword of the Spirit, which is God's word.*
>¹⁸*With every prayer and request, pray at all times in the Spirit, and stay alert in this, with all perseverance and intercession for all the saints.*

PORE AND PARAPHRASE

GROUP DISCUSSION
■ *How often do you consider you might be living in spiritual warfare? what piece of armor do you need to remember to put on?*

PULL OUT

POSE

PLAN AND PIN

What type of "readiness" is required by soldiers who anticipate an enemy that does not engage in open warfare but underhanded schemes (v. 11) and inconspicuous strategies?

LEVITICUS 20:22-24, NLT

22"You must keep all my decrees and regulations by putting them into practice; otherwise the land to which I am bringing you as your new home will vomit you out. 23Do not live according to the customs of the people I am driving out before you. It is because they do these shameful things that I detest them. 24But I have promised you, 'You will possess their land because I will give it to you as your possession—a land flowing with milk and honey.' I am the LORD your God, who has set you apart from all other people.

PORE AND PARAPHRASE

PULL OUT

POSE

PLAN AND PIN

What "customs of the people" have I begun to live according to?

Have full allegiance to God and His purposes

Jesus to the disciples

LUKE 9:23-25, ESV

23He said to all, "If anyone would come after me, let him deny himself and take up his cross daily and follow me. 24For whoever would save his life will lose it, but whoever loses his life for my sake will save it. 25For what does it profit a man if he gains the whole world and loses or forfeits himself?"

PORE AND PARAPHRASE

PULL OUT

POSE

PLAN AND PIN

Joshua's challenge to the children of Israel

JOSHUA 24:15-24

15"If it is disagreeable in your sight to serve the LORD , choose for yourselves today whom you will serve: whether the gods which your fathers served which were beyond the River, or the gods of the Amorites in whose land you are living; but as for me and my house, we will serve the LORD."

16The people answered and said, "Far be it from us that we should forsake the LORD to serve other gods; 17for the LORD our God is He who brought us and our fathers up out of the land of Egypt, from the house of bondage, and who did these great signs in our sight and preserved us through all the way in which we went and among all the peoples through whose midst we passed. 18The

LORD drove out from before us all the peoples, even the Amorites who lived in the land. We also will serve the LORD, for He is our God."

[19]Then Joshua said to the people, "You will not be able to serve the LORD, for He is a holy God. He is a jealous God. ...

[20]If you forsake the LORD and serve foreign gods, then He will turn and do you harm and consume you after He has done good to you." [21]The people said to Joshua, "No, but we will serve the LORD." [22]Joshua said to the people, "You are witnesses against yourselves that you have chosen for yourselves the LORD, to serve Him. ...[23]Now therefore, put away the foreign gods which are in your midst, and incline your hearts to the LORD, the God of Israel." [24]The people said to Joshua, "We will serve the LORD our God and we will obey His voice."

PORE AND PARAPHRASE

PULL OUT

POSE

PLAN AND PIN

> Arise, shine, for your light has come, and the glory of the LORD has risen upon you. Isaiah 60:1, ESV

More Conversation Starters

Deuteronomy 12:2-3; 13:12-18; Ruth 1:11-16; 1 Kings 18:21; Matthew 4:20-22; 6:24; Luke 18:31-33; John 4:34; 17:4; Romans 12:1-2; Ephesians 5:8,14; Philippians 1:21; 2:30; 1 Thessalonians 5:8; 1 John 1:7.

FROM APATHY TO ACTION

Nehemiah's example of active determination

NEHEMIAH 1:3-6,11, ESV

³They said to me, "The remnant there in the province who had survived the exile is in great trouble and shame. The wall of Jerusalem is broken down, and its gates are destroyed by fire."

⁴As soon as I heard these words I sat down and wept and mourned for days, and I continued fasting and praying before the God of heaven. ⁵And I said, "O LORD God of heaven, the great and awesome God who keeps covenant and steadfast love with those who love him and keep his commandments, ⁶let your ear be attentive and your eyes open, to hear the prayer of your servant that I now pray before you day and night for the people of Israel your servants, confessing the sins of the people of Israel, which we have sinned against you. Even I and my father's house have sinned. ¹¹O Lord, let your ear be attentive to the prayer of your servant, and to the prayer of your servants who delight to fear your name, and give success to your servant today, and grant him mercy in the sight of this man." Now I was cupbearer to the king.

PORE AND PARAPHRASE

PULL OUT

POSE

PLAN AND PIN

Notice Nehemiah's immediately sensitive and actively prayerful response to the need of his people. Is my heart sensitive to the needs of God's people (missionaries, ministers, those in need)? What need has God opened my spiritual eyes to "see" and caused my heart to feel passionate about recently? How has my response compared to Nehemiah's?

Joshua's example of active obedience

JOSHUA 3:1-5, NLT

¹Early the next morning Joshua and all the Israelites left Acacia Grove and arrived at the banks of the Jordan River, where they camped before crossing. ²Three days later the Israelite officers went through the camp, ³giving these instructions to the people: "When you see the Levitical priests carrying the Ark of the Covenant of the LORD your God, move out from your positions and follow them. ⁴Since you have never traveled this way before, they will guide you. Stay about a half mile behind them, keeping a clear distance between you and the Ark. Make sure you don't come any closer."

⁵Then Joshua told the people, "Purify yourselves, for tomorrow the LORD will do great wonders among you."

PORE AND PARAPHRASE

PULL OUT

POSE

PLAN AND PIN

Compare Joshua's "early rising" to follow God's commands to cross into the promised land with Moses' actions when facing this same juncture in the journey (Num. 13–14). What is my current "river" of impossibility? Whose actions do mine most closely resemble?

Moses' example of active faith

HEBREWS 11:24-27, HCSB

²⁴By faith Moses, when he had grown up, refused to be called the son of Pharaoh's daughter ²⁵and chose to suffer with the people of God rather than to enjoy the short-lived pleasure of sin. ²⁶For he considered reproach for the sake of the Messiah to be greater wealth than the treasures of Egypt, since his attention was on the reward.

²⁷By faith he left Egypt behind, not being afraid of the king's anger, for he persevered, as one who sees Him who is invisible.

> Better a day in Your courts than a thousand anywhere else.
> I would rather be at the door of the house of my God than
> to live in the tents of the wicked. Psalm 84:10, HCSB

PORE AND PARAPHRASE

PULL OUT

POSE

PLAN AND PIN

How did Moses' focus on the invisible (v. 27) and eternal affect decisions he made? How will keeping my "attention on the reward" affect decisions I have to make this week? What might these decisions cost me?

More Conversation Starters
Exodus 24:4; 34:4; Joshua 6:12-13; 7:16; 8:10; 2 Chronicles 29:20; Psalm 119:147; Matthew 5:10-12; Luke 19:41; Hebrews 11:1-3; James 2:26.

Summarize your conversation with God this week. In what specific ways have you been challenged to renew your mind in regard to your identity in Christ? What have you been challenged to "take off" and "put on"? What practical steps do you plan to take to make this happen? What has been the most meaningful day of conversation have you had this week? Why? What verse has stirred the deepest conversation?

GROUP DISCUSSION
- *In what specific ways has the Spirit challenged you to move from apathy to action in your life?*
- *How has your focus changed during the last six weeks? Is it easier for you to study the Bible now? How has your communication with God changed?*

ENDNOTES

WEEK 1
1. *Blue Letter Bible Lexicon* [online], s.v. "akataschetos," 2008 [accessed January 8, 2008]. Available from the Internet: *cf.blueletterbible.org.*

WEEK 2
1. James Strong, *The Exhaustive Concordance of the Bible,* electronic edition (Ontario: Woodside Bible Fellowship, 1996), G373.
2. Ibid., G4413.
3. Marvin Richardson Vincent, *Word Studies in the New Testament* (Bellingham, WA: Logos Research Systems, Inc., 2002), 275.

WEEK 3
1. William D. Mounce, ed., *Mounce's Complete Expository Dictionary of Old & New Testament Words* (Grand Rapids, MI: Zondervan, 2006), 351.
2. Next Bible [online], s.v. "Psalm 44:20," 2005 [accessed January 18, 2008]. Available from the Internet: *net.bible.org.*

WEEK 4
1. Next Bible [online], s.v. "Isaiah 30:1," 2006 [accessed January 8, 2008]. Available from the Internet: *net.bible.org.*
2. Strong, *Exhaustive Concordance,* H8267.
3. Charles Spurgeon, "The Call of Abraham," The Spurgeon Archive [online], 2001 [accessed January 8, 2008]. Available from the Internet: *www.spurgeon.org.*

WEEK 5
1. John F. Walvoord and Roy B. Zuck, eds., *The Bible Knowledge Commentary: An Exposition of the Scriptures, New Testament Edition* (Wheaton, IL: Victor Books, 1985), 680.
2. Ibid.
3. Strong, *Exhaustive Concordance,* G4161.
4. Bruce Barton et.al., *Life Application New Testament Commentary* (Wheaton, IL: Tyndale House, 2001), 440.
5. Walvoord, *Bible Knowledge Commentary,* 237.

WEEK 6
1. Francis A. Schaeffer, *The Great Evangelical Disaster* (Wheaton, IL: Crossway, 1984), 141.
2. Hampton Keathley IV, "Haggai," Bible.org [online], 2007 [accessed January 16, 2008]. Available from the Internet: *www.bible.org.*
3. Ralph Gower, *The New Manners & Customs of Bible Times* (Chicago: Moody Press, 2005), 294.

ABOUT THE AUTHOR

Priscilla Shirer is a Bible teacher whose ministry is focused on the expository teaching of the Word of God to women. Her desire is to see women not only know the uncompromising truths of Scripture intellectually but experience them practically by the power of the Holy Spirit. Priscilla is a graduate of the Dallas Theological Seminary with a Master's degree in Biblical Studies. For over a decade she has been a conference speaker for major corporations, organizations, and Christian audiences across the United States and the world.

Priscilla is now in full-time ministry to women. She is the author of *A Jewel in His Crown, A Jewel in His Crown Journal, And We Are Changed: Transforming Encounters with God, He Speaks to Me: Preparing to Hear from God,* and *Discerning the Voice of God: How to Recognize When God Speaks.*

Priscilla is the daughter of pastor, speaker, and well-known author Dr. Tony Evans. She is married to her best friend, Jerry. The couple resides in Dallas with their two young sons, Jackson and Jerry Jr.

Jerry and Priscilla have founded Going Beyond Ministries, where they are committed to seeing believers receive the most out of their relationships with the Lord.

Check out Priscilla's other Bible studies
to continue your conversations with God.

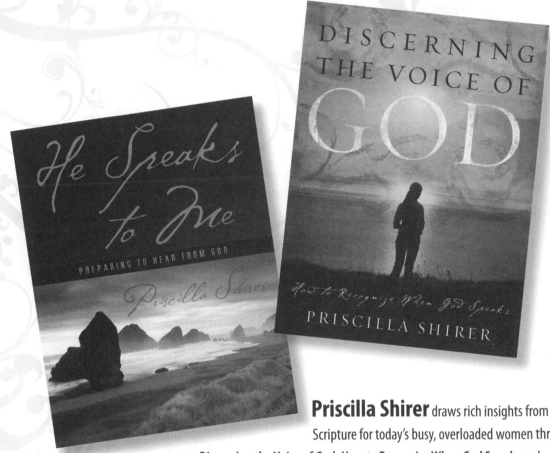

Priscilla Shirer draws rich insights from Scripture for today's busy, overloaded women through *Discerning the Voice of God: How to Recognize When God Speaks* and *He Speaks to Me: Preparing to Hear from God*. These inspiring women's Bible studies show you how to truly know God's voice and how to respond in obedience. You'll learn how to distinguish His voice among the other voices that compete for your time and attention. Each video study features Priscilla's compelling messages on DVDs and personal Member Book study. *(6 sessions each.)* To learn more, visit *www.lifeway.com/priscillashirer*.

1.800.458.2772 • LifeWay Christian Stores

www.lifeway.com/women

LifeWay | Wom